# The New Manager's Workbook:

# A Crash Course in Effective Management

Randy Clark

CONTACT THE AUTHOR

Randy Clark

317-306-9713

rclark@randyclarkleadership.com

# Contents

Foreword.................................................................................................................vii

CHAPTER ONE: RECRUITING AND HIRING ............................................................ 1

CHAPTER TWO: TRAINING .................................................................................. 23

CHAPTER THREE: CONDUCTING MEETINGS ........................................................ 35

CHAPTER FOUR: MOTIVATION & TEAM BUILDING .............................................. 47

CHAPTER FIVE: EMPLOYEE REVIEWS .................................................................. 63

CHAPTER SIX: SILO BUSTING .............................................................................. 67

CHAPTER SEVEN: COMMUNICATION .................................................................. 77

CHAPTER EIGHT: GOAL SETTING ........................................................................ 83

CHAPTER NINE: BEHAVIOR MODIFICATION ........................................................ 93

CHAPTER TEN: CONFLICT MANAGEMENT ......................................................... 101

CHAPTER ELEVEN: PROBLEM SOLVING ............................................................. 113

CHAPTER TWELVE: TIME MANAGEMENT .......................................................... 125

CHAPTER THIRTEEN: WHAT IS LEADERSHIP? .................................................... 141

Appendix........................................................................................................... 151

Acknowledgments ............................................................................................ 152

About the Author.............................................................................................. 152

# Foreword

Last week you were just one of the girls or guys, and now you're the boss. What's next? If you're like many newly promoted managers, you performed well in your previous position, but you're not prepared to be THE manager. Years ago, I was promoted from sales to my first management position. I thought managing was about paperwork, planning, counting money, and other mundane tasks. I didn't understand management is 99 percent about people, and the best managers lead people to improvement. I was unprepared for that role, yet I was asked to conduct group meetings, hire, train, and supervise employees. I was told to complete these activities, but I wasn't given training or direction. I wasn't told how or why. It was expected that if I were good at sales, I would be a good sales manager. Really? It was expected somehow — perhaps by osmosis or telepathy — I would know what to do.

My superiors considered my exposure to previous managers (also untrained) to be my training. It wasn't, and unfortunately this "method" of training remains prevalent. Too often, managers will leave subordinates in charge without giving them direction such as checklists, activities, or goals. Or worse yet, they give them tasks without the tools. Recently I observed a new manager, one week in the position, attempting to complete corrective action with a direct report — in a public area. The new manager was only told to complete the corrective action not how (or where) to complete it.

Over the years, I've learned this sink-or-swim system of management and leadership development is all too common. It not only continues to prevail, but it persists in all types, sizes, and areas of organizations. For example, I know a NASA employee who excelled as an engineer, but lacked people skills. He was promoted to departmental manager but given no management or leadership training. If the sink-or-swim method of management development is a large part of your training, then this workbook is your life raft. It's not intended as the definitive management training book. It's intended to keep your head above water and help you understand some of the most common and oft-repeated management tasks you'll be asked to do.

## Where Do You Begin?

You have already begun by picking up this workbook. Through the sheer act of choosing this book, you have shown a desire to improve — to be a better manager, to become a leader. What often separates a manager from a leader, or a poor leader from an outstanding leader is not intent, but knowledge. Are you ready to learn? Here's your first lesson: *You manage projects, but you lead people.*

## How to Use this Book

There are millions of sources available on how to manage and lead, so why one more book? The reason is many are too specific and/or complicated to use as an everyday reference. This workbook is meant to be your basic management and leadership go-to resource. When you're asked to conduct an interview, give a meeting, or complete a corrective action, and you're uncertain how to proceed, this is your guide

Please feel free to read the book from start to finish, or reference it as you take on activities covered in the workbook. This workbook should be used and reviewed as you tackle the various tasks. With that in mind, it can be used in any order, or as needed. For example, if your first challenge is conducting a meeting, use the meeting activities section, so on and so forth.

My intention isn't to limit the workbook to my thoughts — I hope you add to it, make notes all over it, and use it every day. Used regularly and consistently, through your hard work and trial and error, you will learn how to be a great manager.

## What This Book Isn't

This book is about managing people, about becoming a leader. It is not about the day-to-day operations of the organization. It's not about how or when to order widgets, or checking time cards. You should have a procedural manual for that. It's not about legalities, and for the most part, not about human resource policies. Again, hopefully you have policy books and manuals for these categories. This book has been simplified for a reason. This book is not intended to cover every aspect of leadership or management. Instead, it's a crash course for those who have to know how to lead RIGHT NOW.

## I'm a Product of My Experience and So Is This Workbook

Since this workbook is, in large part, a product of my experience — it's also limited by my experience. I (and my editor) have worked to make this accessible to a wide range of new managers regardless of industry, geography, or culture. My background includes retail, sales, production, and operations management. I have managed a large call center, a B2C installation team, a B2B graphics marketing team, and a service department. I've been an Operations VP, Sales Manager, Marketing Manager, and Director of Communications. I've worked with a small marketing team, in HR as a recruiter, and written corporate policy and procedure books. However, chances are I have not worked in your industry or held your position. I may never have had a job description similar to yours, but I did exactly what you've been asked to do — lead people. *Leadership is universal.*

My scope is also limited by geography, although I've worked in Massachusetts, Memphis, and Michigan, I've spent the majority of my career in Indiana. Where you live and work, the culture and the environment may influence perceptions; however, there are certain truths about people regardless of where they live. I will try to share a few of those truths.

# Are You Sure You Want to Be a Manager?

It's important you're completely honest with yourself. Not everyone is cut out to be a manager; if you're not, and you accept the role, you'll likely be an unhappy camper. Review the list below, and ask yourself, "Why am I considering (or in) a management position?" Is it money, power, control, prestige, less work, stress, hours, or demands?

The points listed above seldom inspire a long term and compelling passionate reason to become a manager. Managing people requires leadership, and may be difficult to maintain the motivation to lead unless you possess a true desire to help others. Leaders who put themselves first will have few followers. Leadership is service; it's not to serve you. Truly great managers are great in part because they enjoy helping others. Great managers get a kick out of watching team members grow as part of the team and as human beings. If coaching, teaching, and helping aren't your primary reasons, management may not be your best option. If you're uncertain about your motivation to be a manager, consider your experience. Have you been a helpful teammate? Do you revel in others' successes? Do you enjoy helping others?

Do you believe you're cut out to be a manager? Then let's get started.

### *WARNING*

Before you continue be forewarned — I repeat myself. If this was a cookbook and one or more of the ingredients used in previous recipes were needed in another recipe, I wouldn't omit the ingredient or tell you to refer to the previous recipe; I would list it in a new recipe. Some of the "ingredients" to successful training, conducting meetings, and time management are the same. Goal setting, team motivation, and behavior modification share similar actions. The activities most often repeated are the key ingredients to becoming a successful manager and eventually a leader.

# Recruiting & Hiring

## Chapter One

# CHAPTER ONE: RECRUITING AND HIRING

I mentioned earlier this workbook is mostly not about human resources — mostly. There may be nothing more important than recruiting and building a competent team around you to your success as a manager. I strongly recommend that you do everything you can to be involved in the hiring process. If possible don't leave this to HR alone — they work for you. The best organizations begin by recruiting the best team through best practices. Very few activities in management are as important as recruiting, building, and improving a team. The most valuable commodity any organization has is its people. Being an effective manager may be more reliant on recruiting skills than any other leadership task.

Organizations that develop their hiring and retention competencies will increase their market share as others lose theirs. This is true regardless of unemployment levels. Sound hiring decisions lead to better employees, better product, better bottom line, a better company, and more market share.

**Before discussing whom, where, and how to recruit, let's clarify one point.** If you're a manager, you manage people. Too many managers put recruiting on the back burner because of "more important" tasks. Few activities are more important than recruiting.

- Recruiting doesn't interrupt your day

- Recruiting doesn't interfere with your work

- Recruiting IS your work

The first time you think, "Crap I have to do an interview now." Remember — hiring the best team possible improves your chance of being a successful manager.

Building a Winning Team Begins With:

- A passion for recruiting. Rather than seeing it as a time waster, embrace the chance to offer someone an opportunity and improve your team.

- An understanding that recruiting is more than reviewing resumes. It's looking everywhere recruits may be available and always keeping an eye out for your next recruit before he or she is needed.

- A dedication to improving recruiting skills.

# Where Are the Best Recruits?

Only a few years ago, most employee recruiting was through newspaper want ads, but it's more complicated today. Online job postings and social media have changed the landscape. So...where do you find today's best candidates? You find them the same way you find prospective customers — by learning where they hang out.

## Where Are Your Candidates and How Can You Reach Them?

Where have you found your best employees and how did they find you? If you're uncertain, ask them. Experiment, try several resources and track their success. Here are a few suggestions:

- **Check college career services**. These services offer job postings and recruiting opportunities in specific areas of study. IUPUI Career Services is an example of a University near me. Research the schools in your area you'll learn most offer career services.

- **Place an ad with Indeed.** Most recruiters are familiar with Indeed.com. If you're not you should be. Indeed can be used to narrow searches by location and position. Indeed claims to be "the world's #1 job site," with a quarter-billion users a month, and it only takes minutes to post positions.

- **Contact unemployment offices**. They, along with other government agencies, offer job services, such as the Indiana Department of Workforce Development.

- **Network** on LinkedIn [www.linkedin.com/nhome], Twitter [twitter.com], and Facebook [www.facebook.com].

- **Consider sites such as Monster.com.** These sites charge a fee, but it may be where the best candidates for specific fields are to be found.

- **Spread the word** within your organization; send an email, or add an employment opportunity section to your internal company newsletter.

- **Ask new hires** to refer friends or associates.

- **Check with other department managers.** They may talk to candidates who don't fit their team, but might fit yours.

- **Add recruiting signage** to events including trade shows.

- **Network with contacts** including vendors, customers, your mechanic, a friendly waitress, etc.

- **Plan outside recruiting**. I frequently worked with a sales manager who was out of budget with no funds to place an employment ad, but needed to add a salesperson. Although he was skeptical, he joined me on an outside recruiting exercise. We went to a local restaurant, I handed out cards and introduced myself, (I know this may be over the top, but it does work) I explained we were interviewing sales people and asked if they knew anyone who might be interested. One gentleman answered, "Yes, me." That was 15 years ago; he's still with the company.

- **Keep old applications** and review them when you have a new job opportunity.

- **Put it on your website.** I've been on hundreds of sites that miss this opportunity. We're redesigning our site, and it's one of the features being added. A word of caution: keep it updated with current available positions.

Don't just rely on placing an ad and hoping the right person responds. Use every resource available to get the word out to as many candidates possible.

Any of the methods above may bring some success, but don't limit your search. Try several avenues.

## Whom Should You Hire?

### How Important Is Experience and Knowledge?

Experience and knowledge are useless, if not destructive, without character. Hiring for character takes a tremendous amount of work. It's so much easier to hire for experience because it reduces training, but is it better? Stop and consider: are some of your best employee's people who came to you with little or no experience? Have you worked with experienced and knowledgeable people who caused problems due to poor character choices? Heaven forbid you have an employee who is good at their work, but also is a malcontent. Although they're toxic and poison others, they're listened to because they have work skills.

### If You Want Valuable, Productive Employees, Hire for Character

If you want to build an outstanding organization, hire for character. Hiring for character is hard work because it doesn't begin with the interview. It starts with developing a training system. If you don't have to depend on experience, if you teach the job, you can concentrate on hiring good people. Training is hard work. It starts with a commitment to training and continues with the development of a training program, which I discuss in the training section. My friend Bob competed in martial arts as a young man. He was able to stand on either foot indefinitely and with the other foot kick higher, harder, and faster than most contestants. He was often asked how he accomplished this. His secret? He got up early every morning before his job and practiced. He practiced during lunch. He went to the gym every night. He worked out every weekend. The normal response to the sharing of his secret was, "No really, how do you do it?" Bob is now a very successful businessman, and part of the reason is his commitment to excellence is the same in business. My point is whether you're training for physical competition or hiring for character — it takes a lot of discipline and hard work. The easy way out is to hire for skill. Hiring for character takes a larger commitment. There is no easy way to be exceptional.

# Types of Candidates

A player

B player

C player

The top 10%.

The next 10% that have the potential to be developed into "A" players.

Someone who regardless of training or repositioning will never be an "A" player.

# How Do You Find the BEST Candidates?

I recommend Top Grading [topgrading.com] by Bradford D. Smart, Ph.D. for its hiring philosophy and as a reference for interview formats and questions. The basic idea behind top grading is that, for any position, there are more qualified and less qualified candidates.

The goal of top-grading is to create a team of 100 percent "A" players, through hiring, training, and repositioning. As leaders, we should never be satisfied. We should always be working to improve our team and our teammates by hiring "A" players. The more outstanding members you have on your team, the higher the opportunity for success.

## Getting the Best Recruits in the Door

### How Many Inquiries Do You Want?

When placing an ad, whether it's LinkedIn, a university job board, or CareerBuilder, keep in mind that the content of the ad will directly affect the number of inquiries. The more specific the job ad the fewer responses you'll receive. A generalized ad usually gets more responses. For example, a team leader I worked with ran an ad for a carpenter. The ad listed requirements for the position as, "a late model truck, all tools, five years on the previous job, excellent driving record, credit check, background check, willingness to travel, work weekends," Guess what? There were very few calls, and no interviews. Do you want to eliminate candidates before they respond, or would you rather have more to choose from?

### If You Over-Qualify, You'll Meet Fewer Candidates Face-to-Face

You've placed an ad, and you're receiving emails and the phone is ringing. You'll need to contact the candidate to schedule an interview. Many managers are tempted to over-qualify the candidate when setting an interview time. The purpose of the communication should be to set a time to meet in-person not to over-qualify, possibly eliminating candidates before the interview. The more information you give about the job, the more you may scare a qualified candidate away. This isn't to say you shouldn't disclose requirements of the job such as hours, pay, and primary responsibilities, but keep in mind; you're trying to bring candidates in for an interview. The best coaches build their teams around the strengths of their players while constantly coaching, training, and encouraging. How often does any candidate fit a job description in every way? While you want to eliminate unqualified candidates over the phone — be careful. Rather than eliminating someone because any one part of the position may not be a perfect fit, bring them in, sit down together and explore the possibilities.

- DO eliminate candidates who don't meet basic requirements. This is tricky and will require some thought and consideration. What are the have-to-have requirements for this position? Not necessarily your wish lists of skills, knowledge, and equipment, but what is essential? For example, a driver will need a valid driver's license; a CSR may need specific computer skills, etc.

- Compliment something you like — their experience, time on the job, etc. Putting someone at ease by complimenting them may go a long way to relaxing them to open up with you.

- Schedule interviews ASAP. It's been my experience and personal observation that every day you wait to schedule an interview; there's a 10 percent or more chance they'll not show for the interview. If you haven't experienced this I'm sure it sounds unlikely that someone looking for a job would schedule an interview and then not show, but it does happen. The further removed a candidate is from directly knowing you or your organization the higher the likelihood of a no-show. For example, a referral from a friend, or a vendor are unlikely to no-show, while a candidate from a blind ad who knows little about you has little obligation to honor the appointment. It happens. And the longer you delay the interview, the more chance the candidate will be taken out of the job market.

- Tell the candidate you'll personally visit with them. By making it personal it may instill the importance of the commitment. Record their name, phone number, and email.

I was recently asked, "Why not conduct the first interview by phone?" Granted, occasionally it's impossible to meet face-to-face, which leaves the telephone or video conferencing as the next best thing. Here are a few of the reasons to meet F2F:

- Communication is much more than verbal.

- Candidates may often open up more in person.

- To introduce the candidate to your work environment and culture.

- Give the candidate an idea about the commute.

- It's more of a commitment from the candidate than a call.

# Fielding Employment Ad Calls Script

This simple script may help you qualify basic job requirements without over qualifying. As always modify it to fit your needs.

- This is _____ who am I speaking with please? I see from your resume you _____ (comment on experience, skills, education, or previous positions).

- What do you know about our company? We are a (brief company description).

- The candidate we're looking for is (list the basic requirements). Does that sound interesting to you? (If yes) I'd like to sit down together and explore this further - I have an opening at_____ o'clock tomorrow. Will that fit your schedule?

- May I verify your phone number and email, please?

- (Share something you like about them)

- (Make it personal) My name is _____ I'm going to set that time aside because I want to talk to you myself. I'll look forward to tomorrow.

I've observed team leaders eliminate possibly qualified candidates before they've given them a chance. There's a fine line between qualifying a candidate for the basic requirements of the job and over qualifying candidates. Too often over qualifying becomes an excuse to avoid in-person interviews due to the time and effort required.

## Creating an Interview Profile

Do you know whom to hire? Have you looked beyond specific job skills, knowledge, and education? Have you considered what traits successful employees in your organization share, and what personalities fit your culture? If not, create an interview profile.

### 4-Point Interview Profile
- Work History. What's important for this position? Is it, job stability, time on the job, number of positions, time in between positions, etc.?

- Requirements of the Position. Don't just consider the knowledge, skills, and education required, but the tools, hours, travel, and character traits, which are also specific to the position.

- Shared Successful Traits. What traits do successful current team members share? Is it passion, hard work, enthusiasm, diligence, a sense of humor, a positive attitude? What are you looking for — energy level, attitude, people skills, communication skills, or something else?

After you've answered the questions above, create a simple interview profile to be used as a checklist during the interview. The following is an example:

### Employment History: Job Stability
- Consider the number of jobs, tenure, and the reason for leaving the position.

- Look for gaps in employment and question these gaps.

### Specific Job Requirements
- What skills or credentials are job requirements? This might include professional certification, a college degree or experience.

### Successful Traits: Major Accomplishments
- Ask the candidate to share a goal that has been achieved at school, work, or extracurricular activities. Although extracurricular achievements such as sports, theater, or clubs may not be applicable to the job description, they may show character traits necessary for the position.

- What character traits do your top employees share? Does the candidate share similar traits?

### Observations (Rate them from 1-5)
- Communication Skills: Did the candidate present clear and complete thoughts?

- Energy Level: Were they enthusiastic?

- Sense of Humor: Is a sense of humor important for this role? Did they share a sense of humor, and was it appropriate? Does it fit the culture and position?

- People Skills: Were they open, friendly, and warm towards you? Did they connect in such a way as to seem to be a good fit for the work environment?

- Motivation: Why do they want to work with you? What are their goals? What motivates them?

- Attitude: Were they respectful, honest, and attentive? How did they speak of past positions?

One key to successful interviewing is to understand who and what will serve your organization best. Do you know whom you should and shouldn't hire? Using an interview profile as a checklist or guide will help identify the most competent candidates and the best fit.

# Employee Interview Checklist

Would you take a seat on an airline that didn't use a pre-flight checklist? Dr. Atul Gawande's in The Checklist Manifesto [atulgawande.com/book/the-checklist-manifesto] realized while boarding a plane that he wouldn't fly if checklists weren't completed. He further concluded that surgeons seldom used checklists even with the most intricate surgical procedures. They flew by the seat of their pants. Hiring employees may not be life or death, like a pre-flight or surgical checklist, but it can positively or negatively affect your business. When interviewing applicants, does your organization use an interview format?

*8-Point Interview Checklist*

## 1. Review the Application and Resume

Briefly review information to remind you of their job history, position desired, and qualifications, including schooling, training, and experience. Also, evaluate any criminal history, salary desired, and references. During the review, question incomplete answers and contradictions with open-ended questions. For example, if there are employment gaps, short time on the job, trends in termination, ask why.

## 2. Greet the Candidate

Personally greet the candidate. If the employment application has not been completed escort them to a quiet area to complete the application. Offer refreshments and invest 3-5 minutes to put them at ease with some chitchat, such as weather, etc.

## 3. Use an Interview Outline (referred to as interview profile on pg 13)

## 4. Conduct a Pre-Selection Interview (attached)

An interview is an information sharing dialogue. A pre-selection interview should focus on gathering information to determine if the candidate fits the position and the position fits the candidate. A pre-selection, or screening interview, is used to determine character traits and skills needed for the position while recognizing candidates who should be considered and eliminating those who don't fit. For example, I recently conducted screening interviews for a graphic designer position. First, I met with the candidates and passed them to the design team. I eliminated several; for example, one who said he was looking for was a short-term job to add to his resume in order to apply for a position at an advertising agency. We were looking for a longer-term employee.

### 5. Share the Opportunities

Share success stories of others on your team — especially entry-level employees who have risen from the ranks. Talk about the culture of the company, including training, charitable initiatives, group outings, etc.

### 6. Share the Pitfalls of the Position

Don't downplay this. Tell it like it is. If there is frequent overtime, weekend work, travel, late hours — tell them. No job is perfect, so share the pitfalls. How can a candidate make an informed decision without all the information? If you're unsure of the pitfalls, ask team members currently holding the position.

### 7. Challenge the Candidate

Ask the candidate why they want to work for your company. For example, asking why we should choose him or her over another candidate may show their level of enthusiasm and passion for the position.

### 8. Make a Decision

If it's a multiple interview process, send the candidate home to consider the pitfalls of the position and set a time for him or her to contact you to schedule the next step. Putting the impetus for follow up on the candidate may show the level of desire the candidate has for the position. Hiring someone because *you* want them doesn't mean *they* want the job. Have them call you back to test their commitment.

If a candidate doesn't qualify for the position, don't lead them on. Tell them the truth. You may find it easier to share something you like about them first, and then explain why the position is not a good fit. I've seldom had anyone not appreciate the truth when I've explained why the job wasn't a good fit. I've also had candidates fight for the position, which caused me to reconsider. With this upfront tactic, I'm never inundated with calls or emails from candidates I wouldn't consider for the position. If they contact me, it's because I wanted them to contact me.

If you're unsure and need time to consider if it's a good fit — tell them, and if you can, share your concern. Give them a chance to answer your doubts.

### *Where Will The Interview Take Place?*

Not only should it be conducted in a clean, uncluttered, quiet location, but in an open area. Conducting an interview from behind a desk is not as conducive to open, honest dialogue as sitting facing one another without obstacles between you and the candidate. The best-case scenario is an open honest dialogue between you and the candidate — don't chance affecting open communication by allowing barriers between you and the candidate.

### What Will You Wear?

Back in the day, the interview uniform was a coat and tie, which was inappropriate when conducting interviews for positions that didn't require a coat and tie. Today, business is often less formal and business casual may be desirous. Obviously, don't dress down to the point of reflecting negatively on your organization, but don't overdress and set yourself too far above the candidate. Wearing torn blue jeans while interviewing a C-level candidate is probably as ineffective as wearing a suit and tie conducting an interview for a warehouse position. Either situation may make it more difficult for a candidate to open up to you.

### What Should You Know About the Candidate Ahead of Time?

Be prepared by reviewing resumes, applications, and conducting research before the initial interview. Consider searching social networks for the candidate's profile to glimpse how they present themselves to the world. You should have a good understanding of the candidate's qualifications and experience without passing judgment or forming strong opinions before meeting the candidate.

### Who Should Be Allowed to Interrupt You During The Interview?

I want to say, "no one," but that's not true. Recently, I conducted interviews while waiting for news about my father, who was in the hospital. I left my phone on. I've conducted interviews while waiting for an important client call and took the call. However, don't make it a rule — it should be the exception. Your staff and team should understand not to interrupt you unless it's critical, can't wait, and no one else can handle the interruption.

### How Long Should an Interview Take?

That's a difficult question because the skill sets required for various positions will affect the time needed to gather the information. I conduct most interviews in 30 minutes or less; however, the interview process may consist of several 30-minute incremental steps. Why 30 minutes? If an interview is focused, and the interviewer knows what he or she is looking for, it can be completed in 30 minutes or less. Especially if the interview is character focused — it doesn't take 2 hours to learn if a candidate has basic good character traits and fits your culture. Often interviewers will budget more time than is needed, then fill the time rather than ending the interview.

### When Should the Interview Be Ended?

The interview should end either when it's determined the candidate does not fit the position, or by explaining the next step in the interview process to qualified candidates. I strongly urge transparency in an interview. As I mentioned earlier, the minute it's determined a candidate is not a good fit or doesn't qualify, end the interview by politely telling the candidate why they don't fit. Why waste time — theirs or yours? It's irresponsible and unfair to continue the interview with someone you wouldn't consider filling the opening. Please don't complete an interview then tell an unqualified candidate you'll contact them.

Plan ahead, be prepared, think this through, and you will increase your competency as an interviewer and the quality of candidates you recommend to your organization.

# First Interview Worksheet

This questionnaire is used as a guide. Jot down your responses and notes throughout the interview.

Name _____ Date _____ Interviewer _____

1. What makes you happy or unhappy at work?

_____

_____

2. What was your favorite job? What was your least favorite, and why?

_____

_____

3. What are the top three things you're looking for in a new position?

1) _____

2) _____

3) _____

4. What are the top three reasons you wouldn't accept a position?

1) _____

2) _____

3) _____

5. Overall, how important is money in your decision? What income do you need to survive, what do you want to make?

6. What are your strengths?

_____

_____

7. What character trait would you like to improve about yourself?

_____

_____

_____

_____

8. What motivates you?

_____

_____

9. Tell me about a goal you achieved and how it was achieved.

_____

_____

10. What is your proudest accomplishment?

_____

_____

Notes

_____

_____

_____

_____

_____

# Notes on the First Interview Questions

*What makes you happy or unhappy at work?* It's important to ask these together, not separately. The purpose is to determine if they dwell on one or the other. Candidates, who share more about what makes them happy, have proven to be positive employees. I recall an interview where it was obvious the candidate hadn't been treated fairly by his former employer; however, the candidate never said a harsh word. Instead, he shared what he'd learned, and how great his co-workers were. He became one of the most positive members of our team. Conversely, when a candidate dwells on the negative experiences of previous employment — they may be the root of the problem.

Overall, how important is money in your decision? What income do you need to survive, what do you want to make? This will give you an idea if the pay structure fits the candidate's needs.

*What character trait would you like to improve about yourself?* I've found people who share their areas of desired improvement to be open, honest, and usually easier to train. They want to learn — they want to improve.

### What Should You Give Candidates to Take With Them?

I suggest preparing a packet for qualified candidates to keep, which could include:

- Job description

- Benefit package information, including costs to employees

- Product brochures

- Company awards and PR

- A company newsletter

- Mission, vision, and ethics statements

# How to Avoid Costly Bad Hires

A multi-step interview system is often the best approach to hiring. If the pre-selection interview has been conducted with transparency — meaning, not only discussing the pros of the job, but also the possible pitfalls — the candidate has time to consider the position, conferring with family and friends. The time between the pre-selection interview and the next step allows time to research the following:

- Criminal background, driver's license, and credit history

- Previous employment

- Education

- Personal references

- Social media presence

### Criminal Background and Driver's License

There are many choices available for conducting these searches, including state government services. For example, the Indiana State Police offers limited criminal background checks [www.in.gov/ai/appfiles/isp-lch] and a Driver's license search [www.driverslicensecheck.com/indiana/driver-license-check]. Once an account has been set up, checks can be completed in minutes. Expect to pay $15-$25 for a criminal background check and $7-$15 for license verification. I wholeheartedly recommend the expenditure. I've found backgrounds with every type of felony — convicted embezzlers applying for money handling positions, burglars applying for residential in-home installation jobs, and much worse.

When Kevin Scott, who was previously convicted on federal charges of bank and mail fraud, was hired to head the Indiana State Employee Retirement Fund (PERF), he had access to 200,000 social security numbers and $11 billion in funds, according to the Indianapolis Star [www.freerepublic.com/focus/f-news/733656/posts], "When Scott applied for the state pension job last year, he gave Indiana State Police the Social Security number of a different Kevin Scott to pass his criminal history check."

Why a driver's license check? First, it shows character, or lack thereof. Do you want someone on your team who cannot keep an operator's license? Without a valid driver's license, how reliable will they be getting to work, or working overtime? There are exceptions; public transportation is the accepted mode of travel in many large metropolitan areas, and more people are choosing alternate means of conveyance such as cycling. I'd also advise caution when considering an employee whose only transport to work is a shared ride with another employee. Ride sharing is commendable, but if it's the only option you lose two employees if the driver is unavailable for work.

### Credit History Check

I have only used credit checks with C-level applicants; however, that doesn't mean a credit check [www.nolo.com/legal-encyclopedia/running-credit-checks-applicants-35457.html] couldn't be used for any position. A wise man once questioned why I was considering promoting a team member who had financial difficulties. He asked, "Why would you trust this person with our money when they can't handle their own?"

Having said that, I recommend caution and consideration when reviewing a candidate's credit history — there can be mitigating circumstances, which should be reviewed on an individual basis. When in doubt, seek your attorney's advice.

### Previous Employment Reference Check

When attempting to gather prior employee information, you may find many organizations have policies limiting the information shared about previous employees; however, I've found a few helpful strategies:

- Ask to speak to the past employee's supervisor; they will often know more about the employee and be more candid than HR.

- If the former employer is limited in what they may share try asking, "Would you hire them back?" Follow up with a simple "Why?" or "Why not?" You may be rewarded.

The University of Pittsburgh Medical School has an excellent reference checklist [path.upmc.edu/payroll/documents/refcheck.pdf].

### Education Check

While an education check may not be needed for every job, how often do we assume the educational information on the application is correct without checking it? George O'Leary was hired by Notre Dame University under the pretense of having a master's degree, which he did not. To learn how to check credentials, visit the college's website or contact the registrar office.

### Personal References

The Business Owner's Tool Kit [www.bizfilings.com/toolkit/index.aspx] offers valuable suggestions for conducting personal reference checks, including a reference check by phone. Often people are more forthcoming when asked questions via phone instead of in writing. Although many recruiters don't check personal references, I have gained valuable insight into someone's character, how to motivate them, and how they may fit in the workplace by taking a few minutes to contact personal references.

### Social Media

Reviewing a candidates social media networks may offer insight into their personality, interests, and how they relate to others. Although inappropriate behavior on a social network may not translate into the work place, it certainly is a red flag.

What's the bottom line? Take time for research, and it may save your company thousands lost from a poor hiring decision.

# Use Common Sense When Vetting Applicants on the Internet

After reading several human resource posts urging pre-interview Google searches to qualify employment candidates, I wondered aloud, "What would a recruiter think of MY Google footprint?" Some view this as infringement, while others consider it gathering information to make an informed choice. Setting aside the ethics for a moment — what would a recruiter find if they Googled you? It had been years since I searched my name. I decided to take a look.

There are lots of Randy Clarks to be found on Google. I first appeared on the fourth page. Would somebody looking to learn more about Randy Clark mistake me for the international speaker, evangelist, or songwriter?

**My first piece of common sense advice: Be sure you have the right person.**

I altered my search to my social media handle, @RandyLyleClark. Midway down the first page, Favstar listed my "top tweets." What would a recruiter think of, "Rumor has it MySpace is set to acquire Polaroid for an undisclosed amount." Would they wonder if I was snarky and mean spirited?

**Second takeaway: Take what you find with the perspective of context.**

I found I had been hijacked — sort of. I was being used by a service I had briefly tried and discarded. They SHOUTED: "Randy Clark uses our service!" No. I. Don't. I'd tried the service and found it lacking.

**Third consideration: Just because the internet suggests someone supports, favors, or recommends something doesn't make it true.**

I am fortunate that odious images of me aren't floating around the web-o-sphere. If Instagram had been around 40 years ago, there may have been. However, there is video of me singing in a cornfield; I think I'm funny...but what would a recruiter think?

**Fourth thought: Take what you find with a grain of salt. Most people have done something, silly, weird, or controversial.**

I also found videos, presentations, and blogs that were my work. This was the Randy Clark I'd want a recruiter to find.

**Fifth recommendation: Look for links attributed to the candidate.**

I've conducted a lot of interviews, but I've never Googled a candidate to help me make a hiring decision, nor have I searched social media — other than LinkedIn, and only by invitation. It's not that I believe it's necessarily an intrusion — it's because it's so easy to get the wrong impression.

## What Should You Ask in the Follow-Up Interview?

For most positions, you'll want a follow-up interview centered on the following questions:

- Follow-up questions to determining the candidate's understanding of information previously shared.

- Probing questions about their previous position(s) and how the candidate may or may not fit the culture of your organization.

- Behavioral questions such as, how do you organize your work or what kind of people did you work best with?

With multiple interviews, I recommend multiple managers conduct them. The insights of two managers are usually better than one; I've missed pertinent information about a candidate another interviewer found. I believe the manager who will directly manage the employee should conduct the follow-up interview; this helps the manager bond with the candidate, establishing a direct report relationship.

The purpose of the follow-up interview is to determine if the candidate fits the culture of the company, has the skills to complete assigned tasks, and understands the responsibilities and expectations of the position. Although the first interview should have confirmed whether the candidate fits the hiring profile, it's prudent to check the profile with a few questions such as:

- What's your proudest accomplishment?

- What motivates you (ex: money, recognition, being part of a team, a boss you can talk to, a feeling of accomplishment)?

- What was your most recent self-improvement?

By following up with some of the same questions/topics as the first interview, you may reveal the candidate's understanding of the questions and his or her consistency in answers.

Ask open-ended cultural and behavioral questions:

- What was your favorite job and why?

- What group of people did you work well with in the past?

- What kinds of people did you not work well with in the past? Why? Give me an example.

- What goals can our organization help you achieve?

- Why do you want to work here?

Regardless of the questions asked during an interview process, mistakes will be made. However, by following a system, considering what traits make the best candidate, and following through — the number of bad hires can be limited.


# Second Interview Worksheet

Name _____ Date _____ Interviewer _____

Ask any follow-up questions from the application or first interview notes you are unclear about.

1. How will our organization help you reach your goals?
   _____
   _____
   _____

2. Tell me about major goals you achieved while at your previous position.
   _____
   _____
   _____

3. What responsibilities and opportunities were outlined in the first interview? (What did they retain? What was their understanding?)
   _____
   _____
   _____

4. What are the pitfalls of this job?
   _____
   _____

5.  What was the biggest obstacle you've faced in a previous position?
    _____
    _____
    _____

6.  Tell me about a team you worked with that fit your personality?
    _____
    _____
    _____

7.  Tell me about a team that didn't work well with you?
    _____
    _____
    _____

**Congratulations, you're ready to hire your first team member.** You may not have an immediate need or position to fill, but you're ready when the time comes. I said ready; I didn't say perfect. You're going to make mistakes. I still do, give me a call I'll share a few whoppers I've made. However, if you follow the ideas shared here, you will improve your odds of hiring the best candidate. One of the most important tasks of building a team is finding and hiring the right people. Not just candidates with the requisite skills, but those who fit the team and culture. But hiring the best people for your team is only the beginning. The next step is training them to be the best teammates.

# Training

## Chapter Two

# CHAPTER TWO: TRAINING

Training is the continuing process of raising the competency of individuals and the team through education, instruction and discipline. Achieving your business goals is directly impacted by the team you build through dedicated recruiting and ongoing training.

In this section, we'll explore how to train, types of training, pitfalls to avoid, and more. First, let's start with...

# How Not to Train

**Don't expect everyone to learn the way you learn.** Too many trainers only teach how *they* learn. Too often, when a trainee does not grasp the information, we think less of them (What are you, stupid?). Instead, you should ask yourself, "How can I adjust my training to my student's learning style?"

The three basic learning styles are:

1. **Auditory**: These learners do better hearing instructions rather than reading them often because they depend on their ability to "read" non-verbal communication, tone and inflection, which gives them a more complete understanding of the information.

2. **Visual**: This style of learner needs to see information. Whether it's observing others, watching an instructional video, or reviewing infographics, they get the most out of what they can see.

3. **Kinesthetic or Tactile**: This group needs to do it. If they're not doing it, then they need to take notes, and if they're not taking notes, they're doodling. They learn by doing.

In addition to the three basic learning styles, most individuals use a combination of many learning styles including musical (rhythmic), interpersonal, spatial, logical (mathematical), emotional, and verbal (linguistic) but for our purposes — let's consider the basic three.

Let's begin by learning your learning style. It's the style you will tend to use when you train.

# Do You Know How You Learn?

Brookhaven College has a wonderful Learning Style Modality Test [https://webster.uaa.washington.edu/asp/website/site/assets/files/3104/learning_style_questionnaire.docx], I highly recommend taking the test — it takes about 10 minutes.

**How to use the Brookhaven Learning Style assessment:**

- Complete and score the assessment

- Be aware of tendencies to train to your preferences

- Have all team members take the Learning Style and Modality Test

- Adapt your training to the learning styles of the team

If you don't use a learning style assessment, you can begin to determine how your direct reports learn by asking these questions.

- How have you learned in the past?

- How do you study?

- What training methods have helped you?

- What training procedures have been ineffective?

For example, my modality is kinesthetic. If you tried to teach me a procedure such as navigating new software only by showing me, I would struggle to retain the information. However, if you walked me through it, allowing me to navigate, my retention would be high. The key is finding how individuals learn and applying that information to training.

I received a call last week from a medical facility preparing me for a scheduled procedure. Near the end of the call, while discussing post-op and physical therapy, I was asked, "Mr. Clark, how do you best learn — by watching, hearing, reading, or doing?" I think that's a pretty good start to understanding, don't you?

### Osmosis Isn't the Best Training Plan

Do you truly believe self-training is the best? People may learn on their own without training and direction, but not as quickly, completely, or correctly. I've heard managers say, "I treat them as adults, so they should just do it!" What I hear is, "I don't take the time or have the confidence to give my team guidance and direction." You must **tell, show, do, and review**. If your team could do it on their own, without training and direction, they wouldn't need you! You'd be out of work.

### Don't Lose Your Patience

The average person needs to be exposed to new information **six** times before it's retained. It may not be retained until the **sixth** repetition. After **six** times, it's usually remembered. In other words, after **6 times** it's not easily forgotten. It takes **six** times to retain. **Six times**. Don't expect to train only once.

We've covered a few basic **don'ts**; let's cover some **do's** next.

## How to Train

### Where do you begin?

- Who will participate? Depending on the size of the group, and level of understanding, it's sometimes more efficient to break into sub-groups.

- Where will the training be conducted? It should be clean, quiet, and suited for training with white boards or technology as needed.

- When and how long will the training be? Consider the best times to reduce work production interference.

- What are your expectations? Begin by sharing your expectations of note taking, participation, and questions.

### Preparation

- What do the trainees need to know before the session?

- What would enhance the training?

- What print material or online sources should be given before training begins? Such as, training materials, study outlines, policies, procedures, and product information.

### Soliciting Questions

Questions are *not* an interruption or delay in your training; they're valuable sources of information. Questions offer insight into your trainees' understanding of the material. Let the trainees know you want questions.

- Explain there's no such thing as a dumb question. The only dumb question is the one not asked. If they're unsure, they should ask.

- Try not to show impatience through body language, tone of voice, or your words. The first time you show annoyance or sound condescending when answering a question, the questions will stop. For many, this may be difficult. One method I've used is to make believe I'm presenting to my boss, customers, or an outside group, not my direct reports. I seldom show my impatience when presenting to these groups.

- Let them know their questions give you valuable insight into their understanding and retention.

- Tell them it's just us, so get over the fear of sounding dumb because they asked a question. It's dumb NOT to ask.

- Inform them you'll check their understanding throughout the training by periodically asking "Do you understand?" and if they say yes, you may follow up with "Great, explain it to the group." Be careful, or some may react defensively. To avoid this, I like to share I have frequently nodded my head in agreement when I had no idea what was going on, therefore, missing a learning opportunity by letting my ego or fear get in the way. If you do catch someone, "nodding " in agreement when they're uncertain, thank them for the chance to clarify and share that others in the group have most certainly done the same. Your purpose isn't to call out anyone in front of the group, but to reiterate how important it is to ask questions when clarification is needed. I also find it helpful to blame the lack of understanding or clarity on the trainer, not the trainees. "Hey people, it's my bad, not yours."

- A trainee may ask a question that's ahead of the training; in other words, you're on page five, and they're on page 15. Establish a parking lot of questions, to be set aside until training reaches that point. Share that parking lot questions are excellent, showing a high level of thought and participation by the trainee.

### Participation

Let the trainees know you expect everyone to participate and will facilitate participation in discussions by calling on everyone. Participation includes staying focused and in the moment. Explain that occasionally everyone loses focus, and it's OK to ask for a do-over. The important point is to set the stage for participation by letting everyone know it's OK to say I didn't understand or I was distracted. Wouldn't you rather have a trainee tell you they missed something rather than leave the session without the information or understanding? Inform them they don't have to feel like a naughty child if they need clarification, it's OK to ask.

*Note Taking*

When my friend, Dr. D.M. Bobersky, facilitates a training session, meeting, or discussion, she distributes an outline. She encourages note taking by wandering the room, spot-checking notes, and answering questions.

Inform the group the points that should be noted. It's best to outline these points using a board, sheet, or computer presentation.

If you don't give your expectations for note taking, you may be disappointed. Let them know what you expect.

# How to Train New Hires

The most important thing about training new hires is to give reachable yet challenging expectations and the training needed to achieve them. Several years ago, I was asked to take over the new hire basic sales training for one of the top 50 home remodeling companies in America. Although the company had a competent selection process, the new sales consultants were slow to start selling. Many of the new sales people took a month or longer to make their first sale. Leads were expensive, and unsold leads issued to inexperienced salespeople even more so. This was a problem. The initial basic training program was a week of classroom and field training. It was an okay training plan. What was missing was the expectation to sell, coupled with a training schedule to prepare the new hires to meet the expectation.

One of the first things I told the new trainees was that I expected them to sell on their first day in the field, which would be only their sixth day with the company. I went on to explain I would give them everything they needed, but it was up to them to learn and retain the information. I told them to be successful; they would need to work their tails off. Throughout the training, I tied learning and study to this expectation. Memorizing information, repeating procedures, and studying for a quiz were all tied to the first sell expectation. I attached deadlines to each step of the learning process and encouraged them not to fall behind. I recognized every achievement and tied it back to making their first sale. I conducted the training for several months and over 95 percent of the trainees completed an order their first day in the field. They expected to and were prepared to do so. Eventually, it became a point of pride to be in the first day club.

This example isn't limited to sales. This procedure, with clear goals and expectations for new hires, can be applied to nearly any position and department.

**Keys to success:**

- Give realistic, achievable, challenging expectations.

- Set a time limit for achieving those expectations.

- Conduct the training needed to achieve the expectations.

- Constantly tie the training to the expectations.

- Give recognition for progress toward the expectations.

### Orientation

An initial introduction to the organization's culture, policies, procedures, and expectations should be one of the first training sessions with new employees.

1. Introduce yourself, including your position, background, and time with the organization.

2. Have all trainees introduce themselves.

3. Give realistic but challenging expectations.

4. Conduct a tour of the operation.

5. Introduce key managers and employees.

6. Discuss note taking, questions, and participation expected in training.

7. Present the organization's mission statement, ethics policy, and vision.

8. Review the job description.

9. Review pay plans, bonus structures, and benefits.

10. Explain offenses that lead to termination.

11. Distribute and review handbooks.

12. Review pitfalls and common mistakes of the position. Too often trainers see this as negative, when, in fact, not advising a trainee of potential hazards of the position is unfair. Making your employees aware of these and helping avoid them could be key to securing their success.

13. Offer examples of successful career paths. Part of your job is to paint visions of the possibilities. For those trainees who want to grow, learn, and expand their responsibilities, sharing the successes of others within the organization is important. The bottom line is that growth is up to the individual employee, but knowing it's possible, that others have done it, inspires confidence.

### 9 Steps to Basic Training

1. Warm up the group with general small talk.

2. Give expectations. Outline what, when, and how information will be shared.

3. Review and test the previous day's material, keep quizzes short, simple, and pertinent.

4. Outline what will be covered in the current session.

5. Explain what to do, how to do it, and why to do it as trained.

6. Review tomorrow's quiz. (I give them a copy of the next quiz for preparation.)

7. Ask for questions and discussions.

8. Ask what they considered the most important point of the session.

9. Recognize good behavior.

Repeat these 9 steps every training session

## How to Train: 3 Training Outlines

These training methods have proven to be effective and comparatively easy to prepare.

### Group Role-Play Training Sessions

1. Warm up the group with general small talk (3 to 5 minutes).

2. Explain that the purpose of the session is education.

3. Focus on one key area of improvement.

4. Explain what to do, how to do it, and why to do it as trained. For example, what to do? Build the best widgets in the world. How to do it? By following procedures. Why do it that way? The procedure has been proven to cut down waste and use time and resources more efficiently, which makes you a better widget builder.

5. Have someone competently perform the procedure.

6. Have others repeat the procedure.

7. Look for any opportunity to give recognition and reinforce positive behavior (never reprimand in public.)

8. When the procedure hasn't been completed properly, show how to do it — then ask the group to explain the differences.

9. Have several team members complete the procedure. It's okay to ask for volunteers (often I will inform and prepare team members regarding their participation prior to the training session).

10. Reinforce following the procedure by explaining how it will help them.

11. Get commitments to follow the training.

**Group Fill-in-the-Blank**

Prepare a training sheet omitting key words and phrases.

For example, the following is an excerpt from a training hand-out about delegation:

Provide Your Team with Direction

What_____ (results) are expected?

When is the _____ (deadline)?

What _____ (activities) should achieve the results?

What _____ (authority) has the team been given?

**Fill-in-the-Blank Points**

- Explain the purpose is education.

- Pass out the sheets and lead the discussion.

- As you come to the blanks, let the team attempt to answer.

- Once the correct answer has been stated, by you or the team, have everyone fill in the blank.

- Discuss what to do, how to do it, and why to do it that way.

- Reinforce following the procedure by explaining how it will help.

**Group Survey**

Either prior to or at the beginning of the session, hand the group a training-related survey. Keep the survey simple, use open-ended questions (**who, what, when, where, why, and how),** and limit the number of questions. Examples could be "What is the best way to build a widget?" "What procedures need improvement?" "How can we do this?" "When can we do this?" "Why would we do this?"

- Have the individuals complete the survey.

- Explain the purpose is identifying opportunities to focus training.

- Discuss the survey either in groups or subgroups.

- Recognize training opportunities understanding who needs help with what.

What if your workplace culture doesn't place emphasis on gathering employee input? Then it's time to get it started, and it starts with you. Listen to your direct reports; be open to suggestions and new ideas. And maybe, just maybe, as your team emerges, others in your organization may notice why and how your team has succeeded.

In one of my first management positions, running a retail clothing outlet, our district and regional management teams were closed-minded to anything new. A new district manager was appointed who not only had an open-mind but solicited ideas. Our district rallied behind his leadership and became the most improved district nationally for the company. Many of the ideas and systems, which employees suggested, were adopted nationally. You and your team CAN affect change.

Here's a sample survey, but as always, you may want to adapt the survey to your needs or create your own.

# Training Survey

Trainee Name _____ Date _____

1. What key concept did you take from the training?
   _____
   _____

2. Was the information pertinent, and is it information you will use?

_____

_____

3. What was the purpose of the training?

_____

_____

4. What would you have discussed further?

_____

_____

5. What could have been improved?

_____

_____

6. What topics would you like to explore in the future?

_____

_____

7. What are your assignments?

_____

_____

8. What commitments have you made in regards to using the training?

_____

_____

## Follow Up, Follow Up, Follow Up

The lack of follow-up training seems to be, in my experience a common issue. According to a study by River Parishes Community College [www.rpcc.edu], 50 percent or more of initial training is lost within 24 hours. However, by following up the second day, with as little as 10 minutes of review, the retention nears 100 percent. After 30 days, most people have lost 97–98 percent of the information — unless it has been reviewed. The more it's reviewed, the more it's retained.

**How do you follow up?**

- Quiz the previous day's key points at the beginning of each session.

- Ask for examples of implementing the training in the workplace.

- If possible, meet briefly with each trainee after the training session.

- Continuously repeat the training. Training never ends.

## Is the Training Pertinent?

Training should be useful and support organizational procedures and policies.

- Will it improve the job, results, activities, or team?

- Does the training adhere to organizational policies and procedures?

- When and how will the trainees use this?

- Does the training fit the needs of the trainees?

Because you're passionate about a subject, doesn't mean your direct reports will be. Do they need the information? Is it information they can use? How do you determine if the training is valuable? Ask them.

## Are You Prepared to Train?

The great thing about training is you get do-overs. You don't have to be perfect the first time because training should never end. When you don't achieve the desired results from your training exercise — tweak it. The more you train, and the more you learn about training, the better trainer you will be. Next, let's look at a management task so closely related to training I'm not sure where training ends and meetings begin. Let's review conducting meetings.

# Conducting Meetings

## Chapter Three

# CHAPTER THREE: CONDUCTING MEETINGS

The primary purpose of a group meeting is to prepare your team for the challenges ahead. Secondary purposes of developing camaraderie, encouraging team cohesion, reinforcing education, giving recognition, reviewing plans, and setting policies, are also important. At the end of every meeting, you should ask yourself:

- What was gained from this meeting?

- Did the meeting focus the team on the challenges ahead?

- Was this a valuable use of time?

- What meeting skills can I improve?

As a young man, I sold Volkswagens. I loved the cars and the corporate philosophy. The dealership where I worked held "sales" meetings every morning. Unfortunately, the sales manager used the time to complain. He complained about where cars were parked, keys hung, and brochures stacked. Although these complaints had merit, they didn't prepare the sales staff to greet customers enthusiastically. The appropriate time to discuss these matters would be after the meeting on an individual basis with the perpetrators. This meeting didn't prepare the team to meet the challenges of the day.

## Four Types of Meetings

**Status** — A status meeting is used to stay current on the progress, results, and expectations of projects. Most status meetings should be short and to the point — primarily about the status of projects, and daily activities. It's not best suited for discussing HOW to do it but rather WHAT needs doing, WHO is doing it, and WHEN it will be completed. For example, I've been involved with daily production meetings that included manufacturing, design, installation, and sales teams. In these meetings we discussed who was doing what, who could help who, where we stood on deadlines, and what had changed. Procedural discussions were limited and usually done after the meeting between the parties directly involved. Status meetings should be held at the rate of status change in your organization. If change orders and new projects come in daily then 10-15 minutes may be needed every day. *Tip — Having everyone stand for this meeting helps keep them short and on point.*

**Decision-making and problem-solving** — These meetings, in some ways, are the opposite of status meetings. By their nature, they will be longer and more involved. Using problem solving techniques to identify areas of improvement can help the team establish how to overcome challenges. Brainstorming, involving the entire team in the process, opens up creativity often presenting new approaches, while at the same time, investing the team in a plan they helped develop. Although it may not be a bad idea to schedule regular problem solving meetings, it's not unusual to schedule meetings as needed. *Tip — Part of your preparation should be asking attendees for their input before the meeting, you'll know where they stands and whom you can call on.*

**Vision, planning, and creative** — This meeting type is used to set the course for the organization. Where are we going? What's next? Some companies hold regularly scheduled meetings, monthly, quarterly, or yearly while others share vision and planning as opportunities arise. This type of meeting may be a group input session or a leader may share their vision and plans. Creating a vision team or conducting a SWOT (strengths, weaknesses, opportunities, and threats; pg. 116) analysis are examples of this meeting. *Tip — Assign a meeting note taker. It will be important to follow up on the conclusions of this meeting.*

**Training** — Training meetings include basic training; follow up training, safety, procedural, and policy meetings. They should be continuous, ongoing, and scheduled on a regular basis. The schedule will depend on the level of experience, how often there are procedural changes, required compliance — such as OHSA, complexity of tasks, and how often new hires come aboard. *Tip — Develop and use checklists for these meetings especially those that will be repeated.*

By first understanding the purpose of the meeting and what you want to achieve, you can determine the style best suited to the purpose. For example, attempting to plan in a status meeting or problem solve in a training meeting may lead to a lack of direction, a lot of confusion, and time not well spent. Today in America the majority of employees believe that meetings are a waste time. With a little planning, you can make meetings meaningful and effective.

## How to Conduct 3 Easy Styles of Meetings

There are many approaches towards conducting a meeting. Some styles will fit your personality while others may not. Experiment and learn what works best for you. Let's review three basic meeting styles.

An effective meeting could use any combination of these styles. Some presenters are good with all three, while others struggle with one type, or another. You don't have to be good with all three styles. You could excel at group meetings if you gave nothing but well-planned, well-executed educational meetings.

### Educational Meetings
Educational meetings are the one format that anyone can use. Let's face it, not everyone is funny or motivational, but anyone can share their knowledge. You could exclusively conduct educational meetings

Educational

Humorous

Motivational

and get results. Educational meetings can cover policies, procedures, and training. They can be basic or advanced and new or review. The sky is the limit.

- **Role-Play:** Managers in production, installation, IT, sales, and marketing can use role-play meetings. It's one of the most effective techniques, and it can be used repeatedly. Choose one procedure to improve. Show your team how to perform the procedure correctly, and then allow your team to execute the procedure. Give your team the time to complete the procedure correctly, or plan to continue the meeting at a later time. If individual's struggle — consider planned follow-up training for them. Role-play is not limited to verbal discussions. Be creative; it can be hands-on, such as how to install, repair, create, and more. *(See more on this method under training)*

- **Quizzes:** Keep quizzes simple and on topic. Use what best fits the personnel and material — true or false, multiple choice, or essay.

- **Review Basic Training:** Whatever training material is available, repeat it, repeat it again, repeat it some more, and repeat it often. Did I say repeat it? I believe you'll be surprised and rewarded by discovering what wasn't retained initially.

- **Use Follow-up Training as a Meeting:** Consider this advanced training. Hopefully, you didn't try to cover all contingencies in the initial basic training. You might survey the team to discover where they need help.

### Humorous Meetings

Okay, this isn't for everyone, but it may be easier than you think. The humor must be appropriate and never attacking or downgrading. It should be on-subject. Having fun at work doesn't have to be unproductive. Humor often improves team spirit and enthusiasm.

- **Game Show:** Take any current game show format and replace the questions with questions relevant to your meeting, industry, or organization.

- **Stage a Trial:** Assign an attorney and a prosecutor. You're the judge, and the group is the jury. Try catching people doing things *right*, such as following a procedure. "How do you plea?"

- **Theme Meetings:** Theme around holidays and seasons, dress up for Halloween or hold an era themed meeting. You or one of your team members dress like a prospect or customer and role-play the interaction. Conduct a summer meeting outdoors.

### *Motivational Meetings*

Some leaders are naturals; however, their motivation skills are often due to practice. One of the keys to motivation is not making it about you. Most of us enjoy hearing about ourselves. So, take every available opportunity to recognize positive behavior in others. We all like recognition and hearing our name. Try this, occasionally when you recognize a group or individual, add, "Let's give them a hand!" while applauding enthusiastically.

- **Team Slogans:** At the beginning and/or end of meetings, use a group slogan such as, "Go team," "Team first," or "we're #1," be creative. I know a team of positive producers whose daily end-of-meeting slogan is, "Don't suck!"

- **Call and Response:** Call out questions for which the team has a planned response like, "Who's the best team?" I observed a team that had preplanned responses for each of several products they marketed. Every time a product was mentioned they responded. Some of the responses were rather silly but effectively motivated the team.

- **Rewards:** Show your team the *rewards of excellence*, be it financial rewards, job satisfaction, advancement, etc. Explain the activities needed to excel, and then show your team how it benefits them.

- **Hold a Challenge or Contest:** Contests can be one-on-one or team vs. team. They may be based on quality, production, overall performance, etc. The prize doesn't have to be extravagant; for many, pride may be the best prize of all. Something as simple as a winning ribbon may be more effective than you think. However material rewards don't suck either.

# 13 Steps to Planning a Meeting

We've all been part of unproductive, time-draining meetings. If you conduct meetings, don't be a time and energy vampire.

1. **Plan the meeting.** Have an agenda — know what you want to discuss. Use a meeting outline, scratch it on a legal pad; write it in Word, post it notes, or on your phone. It doesn't have to be fancy or formal to keep you on track.

2. **Follow a schedule**. Have set times and always start on time. Most, but not all, meetings can be accomplished in 20-30 minutes, after which even the most attentive team members may begin to drift.

3. **Don't reprimand**. Never reprimand an individual in a group setting. Never, never, ever — Never. This should be done in private. It's okay to discuss group initiatives that need improvement such as "We've noticed widget production is down" but not, "John and Mary you're production is down."

4. **Avoid lecturing**. Don't stand in front of the group and talk for 30 minutes. Your team will lose focus and concentration. Are you that good of an orator?

5. **Involve everyone**. When planning the meeting consider whom you will involve and how you will involve him or her. Before the meeting, discuss the topic with a few team members. If you like their input let them know they may be called upon.

6. **Be flexible.** Occasionally you may need to adjust your meeting plan to share new information; the key here is that you have a meeting plan. If, however, you're changing your meeting frequently, you may be trying to manage results not activities. You can only change results through planned activities. Results are history, which can be learned from, but until someone invents a time machine, can't be changed. You will not change anything dwelling on results. You must analyze the results to determine the detrimental activities, which led to the results. What activities need improving? Change comes not from listing the results but from changing activities.

7. **Keep control**. Don't allow an individual to dominate the meeting. It's better to politely tell someone who is off subject that their point may be more appropriate for another time, than allow the meeting to be disrupted.

8. **Involve as many senses as possible**. Show it, talk about it, and share it in writing. Consider the varied learning styles of your team.

9. **Use multiple media.** Outside materials, articles, videos, samples, flyers, graphs, and charts.

10. **Involve others**. Share a broader view by inviting members from other departments or organizations to participate. Share a larger picture.

11. **Don't allow interruptions**. Emphasize the importance of being on time. Don't allow tardy people to interrupt the meeting. It's unfair to those teammates who were on time. If six people wait five minutes on another to join the meeting, you've wasted half an hour. "Catching up" someone tardy may be

worse. Do you chance losing your audience during the repetition or paraphrase and shortcut the information? No, ask the tardy person to get back to their duties. This reinforces the importance of being on time, and you can fill them in later.

12. **Eliminate distractions**. Turn off phones and devices except when they're essential to the meeting. It's impossible, for your audience, to give their full attention when distracted by phone, text, email, and social media.

13. **Give recognition.** People want to repeat behaviors that bring accolades.

# How to Outline a Meeting

By creating an outline, you'll have a better idea of what you want to discuss, how long it will take, and who will be involved. Keep in mind, content is what matters, not pretty notes.

Below is a simple meeting outline. Use it, or make your own, what's important is to plan your meeting. Even the best extemporaneous speakers may ramble, lecture, and get off topic without a plan.

- **Choose your subject matter.** For example; review training material, policies, procedures, activities, and results. Recognize exemplary behavior and introduce new products, contests, goals or share inspirational and motivational material.

- **Decide on a meeting style.** Will it be educational, motivational, humorous, or a combination?

- **Implement the style.** It could be role-play, fill in the blank, review?

- **Determine the Key Points?** What should stand out? What should the attendees take away? Most meetings should include activities to improve, continue, begin, or eliminate.

- **Identify team members to call upon.** As I've mentioned, prepare team members by asking a few questions pertinent to the subject matter, before the meeting. This way, you can determine if they're prepared for your questions.

- **Share the benefits.** What will the meeting do for them? Most people are primarily motivated by self-interest. It could be money, recognition, advancement, job satisfaction, workload, or schedule.

- **Plan a commitment.** Ask the team members to commit to following the activities outlined in the meeting. Consider asking what they took from the meeting and how they will use this.

# Meeting Outline

Date _____

Time to Start _____ End _____

1. Subject: _____

2. Style:  _____

3. Activities to improve, continue, begin or eliminate:

_____

_____

_____

4. Teammates to engage:              Subject, question:

_____        _____

_____        _____

_____        _____

5. How this benefits the team or individual team members:

_____

_____

_____

6. Commitment to following the activities:

_____

_____

_____

# Evaluating Your Performance

Improving your presentation skills begins by determining areas with room for improvement.

Ask yourself the following after the meeting:

- What worked and why?

- What didn't work and why?

- What needs improving?

- What was learned?

- Where should focus be concentrated?

- What was accomplished?

For additional input ask a trusted team member, who participated in the meeting, the same questions. Set the tone by explaining compliments, although nice, won't help improve presentation skills — constructive criticism will.

### Manage the Activities, Not the Results

When planning your meeting, keep in mind the results are history — you can't change the past. Hopefully, though, you'll learn from the past. To change the future, you have to change activities. You need to understand what needs improving, as well as, recognize successful activities to repeat. Tie activities to the results expected. Don't allow luck to be credited for success. Seneca, a first century Roman philosopher, said, "Luck is what happens when preparation meets opportunity." When planning the meeting, consider the following:

- Activities to repeat

- Activities to begin

- Activities to improve

- Activities to eliminate

- Activities to reintroduce

Linda Carmady, the past president of the central Indiana Better Business Bureau, had an ingenious solution to a common activity-related problem — successful activities mysteriously being discontinued, in other words sometimes a successful practice or activity just...disappears. Linda instituted a scheduled review of activities. The team would decide if activities were to be continued, thus re-focusing the team on the activities.

## You Want <u>Me</u> to Give a Presentation?

There may come a time where your supervisor wants you to give a presentation to all or part of the organization or even outside of your company to a group or client. If you're like a lot of folks, your first reaction may be profound fear. It's natural. Let's face it: throughout history, having a gathering of humans staring at you was often not a good situation (a gathering of cavemen all staring at you intently most likely meant you had food they wanted or YOU were the food.)

## How to Prepare to Present

### Research

As valuable and accessible as information via online search is; don't end your research there. Seek advice and ask for help. Whom do you know that understands your topic and may offer insight and ideas?

### Outline the Presentation

I'd advise against writing your presentation word-for-word. This adds a level of difficulty, and often comes off stiff and phony. Create an outline, bullet the key points, and add thoughts. Keep it simple.

### Avoid Boredom

Avoid giving a boring lecture by asking questions. Look at every point and ask yourself, "Could this be framed as a question?" Use open-ended questions to solicit thorough answers. By asking attendees questions before your presentation, you may identify whom to call on.

### Tell Stories

Give examples, personal experiences, and third-party stories. Don't tell jokes unless they're appropriate, and you're good at it. A funny story, with a point, trumps a joke any day.

### Use Multimedia

Use a simple PowerPoint (or Prezi), a white board, or video. Don't downplay handouts; fill-in-the-blank and action plans can engage the audience.

### Practice

Practice, practice, practice, practice, practice, and practice — I can't say it enough. The best way to overcome fear of failure is preparation. Don't just practice until you get it right — practice until you can't get it wrong. Turn off your music while driving and practice. Turn off the TV and practice, present to your kids, your partner, a recorder, and practice in front of a mirror. Practice!

## Ready, Set, Go!

Here are a few tips to remember when it's time to present:

- Everyone has jitters. You're not alone. I haven't met a presenter who doesn't get some jitters before, during, and after presenting. The more you present, the easier it gets.

- Nothing beats preparation. If you've practiced, you will be much better than if you haven't.

- You will mess up. You'll omit, forget, and ramble. It's no big deal, unless you make it one. Your audience doesn't know so don't tell them. Don't apologize for your mistakes.

- Take deep breaths and look in the direction of the audience — even if it's a spot on the wall and smile.

- Call on others — they can help, especially if you need to pause to gather your thoughts.

If you're prepared and you take the time to practice, presenting can be a fun, rewarding, and fulfilling experience. Presenting can be used to advance organizational initiatives to employees, prospects, clients, and vendors.

## Other Meeting Points

### Don't Lecture — Plan Engagement

A common meeting mistake is lecturing, as in, talking *at* the audience, not *with* them. Most of us are not sufficiently engaging and entertaining enough to hold the team's undivided attention for 30 minutes of chatter. Have you been on the other side of one of these lectures? Were you bored? Did you drift off? Learn to use questions instead of statements. Instead of lecturing about how a thing-a-ma-jiggy is made, *ask* someone how it's made. Instead of reading through the manual, ask someone the points in the manual. Learn to use open-ended questions. **Who? What? When? Where? Why? How?**

*Choose Your Audience*

An installation manager planned a weekly crew leader meeting around a reoccurring problem. The problem was caused when specific procedures weren't followed. He'd discussed this subject previously, and it was becoming difficult to keep this topic positive. I asked how many crew leaders didn't follow the procedure, and he said, "two." Don't give a meeting to everyone when it's only aimed at a few. This will be negative, boring, and for many, a waste the time. Conduct a separate meeting for the offenders. Don't waste the time of those who do it right, work with those who need the help.

# I Think I've Said This Before…Sound Familiar?

Don't be afraid to repeat meetings. You should PLAN to repeat meetings. Most people won't get it in one meeting. It's good to repeat — it will improve your team. You don't have to come up with something new every meeting. Having said that, don't conduct a meeting just to have a meeting. Repetition of any meeting is acceptable but only if it is needed.

**One last thing — There's a secret to giving successful meetings. Do you want to know what it is?**

It's not a secret because I just mentioned this. The secret is - practice. To this day, I isolate myself and rehearse meetings, and I've conducted meetings for…a long time. Practice. When you mess up, don't give up. You're going to make mistakes. Practice and you will improve. So far, we've recruited, hired, and trained our direct reports. Let's see if we can't build them into a cohesive team and learn what motivates them.

# Motivation & Team Building

## Chapter Four

# CHAPTER FOUR: MOTIVATION & TEAM BUILDING

Inspiring team members to put forth more effort and determination then they would without your influence not only increases performance and production, but improves job satisfaction, which increases retention. To do this, you must determine what motivates each person on your team. Everyone is different, and many will combine various types of motivation. If you want to understand their motivation, ask, observe, and remember.

## How to Motivate Others

The first key to motivating anyone is to understand what motivates him or her. Too often, well-intentioned leaders attempt motivating their team with what works for them, not necessarily what works for others.

### What Motivates You Isn't Universal

In a previous position, I once told the president of the company I was more motivated by recognition and a sense of accomplishment than by money. Rather than use this information to his advantage in motivating me, he eliminated my bonus plan. Money was one of his key motivators, and he expected others to be the same.

Don't assume everyone is motivated by money. Managers are frequently surprised when added financial incentives (bonuses, etc.) don't motivate employees to accomplish more. Money may limit de-motivation, but it's often not the best incentive. In a Forbes post, Money Is Not The Best Motivator, Jon R. Katzenbach and Zia Khan [www.forbes.com/2010/04/06/money-motivation-pay-leadership-managing-employees.html] explain how, "Less costly kinds of encouragement can be far more effective." Recognition, an open door policy, creative freedom, being an integral part of a team, and flexible hours can all be highly effective low cost motivators."

### Using Fear to Motivate

Fear, as a motivator, isn't as effective as many believe it to be. Unfortunately, motivation through fear may bring results, but if used repeatedly, it will destroy the environment that allows teammates to become self-driven, and will lose its effectiveness.

### Give Your Team Tools, Guidance, and Direction

Direction motivates employees. Sharing what your direct reports need to succeed is highly motivating. If you've ever worked without direction, you understand how de-motivating it can be. Written policies and procedures, company goals, visions, missions, and ethics policies all define the organization and give employees a working framework. Give your team a road map. Be their compass.

Don't confuse direction with micro-managing. People need room to be creative and the opportunity to be entrepreneurial. Effectively executed individual and team goals inspire and motivate — especially if they align with personal life goals. Asking someone to complete any task without the proper tools isn't de-motivating, it's destructive. Give your team the tools they need and one of those tools is direction.

### Staying informed of Evolving Motivators

Staying informed of what motivates your team is fluid, as goals change over time. For example, an unmarried employee's motivation may change if they wed, and will likely change again if they have children. Keep in mind, the employee's motivation may change at any time. It's an ongoing process.

## Improving Employee Morale When It's Tough Going

The economy has been a roller coaster the last couple of decades. Even when it seems to be going well, many are waiting for the next fall. During challenging times when the economy is fragile, positions may be eliminated, and often the remaining employees are asked to do more without added compensation. At times such as these, morale is more important than ever. Improving morale when people are given more responsibilities, raises are non-existent or minimal, and many are concerned about their future — is tough, but it can be accomplished. Remember, employees **can** be motivated during challenging times.

## Where to Begin

You improve morale when you give direction to your team. Consistent routines without revolving door changes, combined with plans of action will improve morale. Show your team how to get things done, and they will cherish the achievement.

### Share the Love

We all desire more recognition, yet we don't always do a good job of giving recognition to our team. I cannot tell you how many times I've heard a manager brag on one of their people to find out they've never told the employee.

### The Power of Praise

In a recent survey of administrative employees [www.tlnt.com/2012/04/19/retaining-employees-research-shows-its-all-about-recognition-done-right], 66 percent said they would leave their current position if not shown appreciation by their manager. Praise can be one of the truest forms of appreciation.

I've seen various surveys over the last three decades demonstrating the power of praise in the workplace. I'm often met with doubt when I claim recognition to be the number one factor in retaining or losing valuable employees. Many managers believe money is the prime motivator for most employees, and while that may be true for the underpaid and truly money motivated, for most, praise is a more powerful incentive. Ask yourself this — have you ever accepted or kept a job that paid less than another opportunity? If you have, then money wasn't your primary motivation. Has praise and recognition, being part of a team, a fun work environment, and interesting work been more important to you than money?

In Leigh Branham's book, "The 7 Hidden Reasons Why Employees Leave," he says —

> *"Employees need to feel a sense of worth. Feeling confident that if you work hard, do your best, demonstrate commitment and make meaningful contributions, you will be recognized and rewarded accordingly."*

# 5 Ways to Give Praise

- **Praise activities,** not just results. By recognizing positive activities, regardless of the results, you not only show understanding and involvement, but you're also reinforcing the behavior.

- **Praise character** — Praise who someone IS, not just what he or she does.

- **Praise soon and often** — If the employee has done something praiseworthy, do it as close to the event as possible. If your praise is real, from the heart, and founded in fact, you can't give too much praise.

- **Praise in front of peers** — If you really want to show your appreciation, give it an audience. But also know your teammate — not everyone enjoys the attention.

- **Praise in writing** — Write a thank you note, send an email, or mail a card.

How important is praise at work? When praise is missing from the workplace, a majority of employees will consider leaving to find it, and even if they stay, it can negatively affect performance and production. Losing valuable employees is painful. Finding replacements and training them is costly. Losing the personal connections made in the work place takes a toll. If you want to put a dollar figure on it, you can. According to President of Bliss & Associates Inc., William G. Bliss, the cost of employee turnover is close to 150 percent of the employee's annual salary [see www.alexanderporter.com.au/wp-content/uploads/2015/07/The-Cost-of-Employee-Turnover.pdf].

Do you give praise as often as you should? Do you share recognition whenever it's deserved? If not, let's make a commitment to give more praise.

Give praise every day and your best people will stay.

## 15 Motivating Tips

1. Begin an "I caught you board" where anyone can "catch" another employee doing things right.

2. Volunteer to support a charity as a team.

3. Involve team members in planning.

4. Supply employees with the tools they need to get the job done.

5. Have an open book policy; honestly share the state of the organization.

6. Offer flex schedules, time to put the kids on the bus, or time to take a class.

7. Ask for opinions and advice from employees and use it.

8. Offer a performance bonus based on improving net profit. A win — win.

9. Start an internal newsletter focused on positives in the organization.

10. Recognize an employee in every issue of the company newsletter.

11. Recognize employees' positive behavior and contributions at meetings and company functions.

12. Leave a positive note on a team member's check stub.

13. Add non-traditional benefit options such as wellness programs.

14. Hold occasional team meetings in an open "let's talk" round table forum.

15. Create a one-page handout titled "Another Good Job" and recognize all departments and team members involved.

## Do You Know What's Important to Your Employees?

How can you make your business a better place for your employees? You can start by conducting an employee survey. As surveys are completed you'll uncover trends, ideas, and surprises.

The purpose of the survey is to identify areas for workplace improvement. Use the information accordingly. Conducting the survey anonymously, with no repercussions, solicits transparent and truthful responses.

### *Set the Stage*

- Reassure employees that the survey is anonymous.

- Explain the survey is to help improve the organization.

- Make it clear that honest answers are appreciated.

- Caution employees not to over-think answers; their first choice is often the best.

# Motivator survey

Rate the following motivation factors. The factors listed below aren't all-inclusive and are in no certain order. Consider what motivating factors might enhance or improve performance. For example, someone may not consider accepting a job without health benefits; however, including health insurance in a benefits package may not motivate an employee to improved performance. Whereas someone working without health benefits, upon receiving benefits, may experience improved performance knowing the organization has taken a vested interest in them.

**1 = always, 2= usually, 3 =sometimes, 4= seldom, 5= never**

1. Recognition, being recognized for effort, character or results. _____

2. Having a leader you can talk to and share with _____

3. Prizes, trips, and rewards _____

4. Money, incentives, bonuses, the opportunity for additional income _____

5. Competition between teammates and/or other teams _____

6. Family time, self-time, flexible scheduling, extra free time _____

7. Opportunity to advance and grow with the organization_____

8. Continued education, either formal or in-house _____

9.  Benefits, health, insurance, retirement plans, etc. _____

10. A sense of accomplishment when projects are successful _____

11. Being an integral part of a team. Feeling like you are "in on things" _____

12. Nontraditional benefits such as, wellness programs, gym memberships, or day care _____

**Other factors**

_____
_____
_____
_____
_____

# Company Improvement Survey

If you could change or improve one thing to make your work more efficient, enjoyable, or easier, what would you change?

_____
_____
_____

If your supervisor asked you how they could be a better supervisor, what suggestions would you offer?

_____
_____
_____

What do you believe is the best thing about working here?

_____
_____
_____

What is the worst part about working here?

_____

_____

_____

What is most important to you in the workplace?

_____

_____

_____

What else would you like to share to help us make this a better place to work?

_____

_____

_____

_____

Gather and review the surveys looking for trends, ideas, and suggestions to improve your organization —
then do something about it.

## Know When to Ask

Tell don't ask, is an old school management technique that never was the most effective method for many
situations. Following orders, while necessary in some disciplines, stifles creativity, limits dialogue, and elimi-
nates brainstorming. If you want your team to embrace initiatives, the first step is to engage and involve
them.

Before conducting a seminar on teamwork at a retail outlet, the General Manager told me it was difficult to
get people to work outside of their department. The GM went on to share that employees are informed
they're paid to work wherever they're needed — not only their department. I asked the GM if the
employees had ever been asked how helping other departments could be advantageous to them. During
the presentation I asked the following:

- How could interdepartmental help positively affect the customer experience?

- How could a poor customer experience affect the bottom line?

- How could lost revenue impact an individual employee?

The staff responded that helping from one department to another could make a huge difference for the customer. Although this retailer has three distinct departments that's not how the customer views it. If a customer needs help they don't care what department an employee is assigned to — if an employee is available the customer expects their attention. The team went on to share several reasons they should help each other including how service could affect bonuses. When the retail staff was asked to share their ideas they not only gave the management team a few thoughts to consider, but also made improving interdepartmental teamwork their idea. Only two days later, department managers and employees had put interdepartmental action plans in place to help each other.

Before you decide to use the BIS method (because I said so!) or the old "my way or the highway" approach, consider whether involving the team by asking for their input is a more effective way to accomplish the desired end result. If laws and compliance regulations, policies and procedures, and proven systems aren't being ignored or circumvented, asking brings a greater buy-in than telling.

## Improving Your Team — Is It Process or Procedure?

When results aren't achieved, managers often jump to conclusions before gathering and analyzing information. I've seen procedures changed that weren't being followed, and processes (the act of completing procedures) micromanaged when the procedure itself was flawed. Both resulted in little or no improvement.

I worked with a company with a simple procedure for answering web inquiries. When a new inquiry was submitted, the response team was sent an email and was to respond within 10 minutes. It was discovered some responses took up to an hour. The IT team was tasked with improving the system. After spending hours "improving" the system, the results didn't improve. It wasn't due to the procedure; it was process. The team responsible for answering the inquiries only checked their email once an hour.

**How would you answer these two scenarios? (Full disclosure: It's a trick question.)**

*Scenario I*

You make widgets. They haven't changed, and nothing out of your organization's control is affecting production, however, production has declined. Is the cause process, defined as how the team works together or procedure? *Answer below.*

## Scenario II

You offer a service. The sales team is responsible for driving sales. The personnel haven't changed, and economy is the same. Sales are down 10 percent from the previous year. Do you need new sales procedures, better processes, or new sales people?

## The Answer

By now you've figured out — there is no good answer because you don't have enough information. But too often management decisions are made without proper research. Facts need to be gathered and analyzed before taking action. Begin by looking at process and procedure. Management's first reaction shouldn't be to jump to conclusions and alter procedures (or processes) without understanding why it didn't work in the first place.

# Four Conditions of Process and Procedure

  Working process and working procedure

Working process with a <u>flawed</u> procedure

 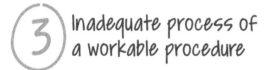 Inadequate process of a workable procedure

Inadequate process and a <u>flawed</u> procedure

1. The team is on track. Reinforce this positive behavior with recognition and rewards.

2. If the process is good, but the procedure is flawed, ask the team to give suggestions to improve the procedure. Review the team's goals, refocus priorities, and assign tasks with the best opportunity to improve the procedure. Establish and train the new or improved procedure.

3. If the process is inadequate, but the procedure is workable, what steps in the process need improvement? Where is the process faltering? Are procedures being followed? Have they been adequately trained? Follow through with training and/or corrective action as needed.

4. If process and procedure both need improving, you have your work cut out for you, but the good news is you can make a tremendous impact. Start by focusing your team on the procedure. The

process of working together to improve the procedure may improve their teamwork. Once there is a consensus on the procedure — begin analysis of the process. How can it be improved? Where is the training needed? Do you have the right people for the tasks?

## Building a Great Team

Great teams are built; however, they're seldom built overnight, and are often created through trial and error. So... how is a great team built? It begins with the interview process by hiring people of character who fit the culture, and fill a role on the team. Hiring for knowledge or skill, without considering character, often leads to problems. Poor character may lead to poor choices, which can and will disrupt the team.

- **Culture** — Someone who doesn't fit the culture may become unhappy, which hinders team development. For example, your team loves cats, and you have an office cat — someone who hates cats will not fit in.

- **Skills** — Roles must be filled. A baseball team made up of all pitchers, regardless of how well they may throw the ball, will not succeed.

- **Training** — Without a commitment to ongoing training and development, it will be difficult to build a great team.

Instilling the team with a sense of ownership leads to greatness. It's their job, department, and company as much as anyone's. Great teams initiate tasks and find solutions because they've been empowered to do so.

Training should include more than work related tasks and systems — it should include team dynamics, communication skills, brainstorming, conflict resolution, and more.

The most attractive leaders, who build great teams, do all of the above. Great leaders share a vision by involving the team in the vision; the vision becomes the team's vision.

## What Is a Team?

A team is an organized group of people who hold themselves accountable for achieving clear, definable, objective goals. A successful team, working together, will achieve more than what could've been achieved individually. Below are 13 steps to building a great team:

1. Hire for character over knowledge and skill.

2. Search for "A" players who fit the culture.

3. Fill roles and position team members where they may excel.

4. Commit to constant, ongoing training.

5. Involve the team in decision making.

6. Empower the team with motivating tasks that have clear, visible outcomes.

7. Develop a sense of team ownership.

8. Delegate authority and responsibility.

9. Be a leader teammates can talk to — be a good listener.

10. Lead by example.

11. Give recognition and credit where it is due.

12. Share visions, paint dreams.

13. Be supportive, not defensive.

## 11 Steps to Team Success

How can an existing team improve? If you're part of a team, what can you do to help it become a better team? Here are a few thoughts.

1. Work hard, individually and collectively.

2. Define team goals as a group.

3. Help each other.

4. Be the best teammate you can be.

5. Practice active listening by being attentive, listening without prejudice, and focusing on what is being said not what you want to say.

6. Be time considerate, be on time, and remember the value of others time.

7. Be considerate of others — convey respect.

8. Be open and supportive. Don't react defensively.

9. Be sensitive, understanding, and empathetic.

10. Share excitement and give praise.

11. Be responsible and take responsibility.

Have you been part of a great team? What made it great? What did you learn? What can you copy? What role did you play in the team's success? Have you been involved with an unsuccessful team? What made it so? What should you avoid? Your answer to improving your team may lie in these answers.

## How to Help Your Team One Member at a Time

- **See more in people than they see in themselves** — When you recognize the potential in others that they don't see in themselves, and help them achieve their potential, you become a life changer.

- **Share what you know** — Share your knowledge. Train, teach, present, and offer to meet one-on-one.

- **Share what you've learned** — Let others know your successes, but more importantly, your mistakes. Give others a chance to learn from your miscues. Inform them of pitfalls, roadblocks, and challenges.

- **Keep an open mind** — You may not have the best or only thought. Support the initiatives of others.

- **Be a mentor** — Take people under your wing. Help others get what they want by giving them what they need. Elevate those around you. Share your talents, give your heart, be courageous, and make a difference.

## Having Fun at Work

### What is fun at work?

One, often overlooked, aspect of workplace fun is getting the job done. The pride of successfully completing tasks and the attached feeling of accomplishment is F.U.N. Remember back in school when you didn't study for an exam, because you had something "FUN" to do instead? The next day, with an upset stomach and sweaty palms, you tried to fake your way through the test and failed miserably? Remember that? How fun was it? When we succeed, we feel better about ourselves. It's certainly more fun than the alternative.

You don't have to play to have fun at work, but you can. Throw a Frisbee, play a joke, socialize a little. When you make work fun it energizes the team, produces endorphins, and stimulates production. A video production team I work with has an office full of Nerf machine guns, catapults, and rapid-fire shooters, which may burst forth at any time. Their project tracking board is made up of…Legos. Do you think most days their team enjoys coming to work? I do, and I know it positively impacts their performance.

### How important is having fun at work?

A positive and fun environment often leads to:

- Increased productivity

- Lowered absenteeism

- Improved job satisfaction leading to employee retention

OK, OK… You said you were gonna tell us how to make work fun.

## How to Make Work Fun

### Constantly give recognition for achievement, activities, and character.

Offer congratulations in front of peers. Give recognition to the team. Write a thank you note, send an email, or leave a voice mail. Once, at a company function, I recognized a teammate's dependability. His wife called and thanked me. She knew he was dependable, yet no one had ever recognized him. Tell me that wasn't fun. Don't limit the recognition to results. Sometimes recognizing positive activities not leading to the desired results is more meaningful. You may think, well that's nice, but how is it fun? It's certainly fun to be on the receiving end and it can put a smile on the face of the giver, as well… And that's fun.

### Involve everyone, make them part of the team.

Be a great teammate. You don't have to be best friends, but you should be an understanding teammate. Listen without prejudice, accept idiosyncrasies, solicit ideas and ask for help. Be a teammate, or boss, people can talk to. Be someone who will listen with an open mind. Having teammates who respect one another is a heck of lot more fun than the opposite.

### Create a fun work environment.

One company I work with has floor to ceiling graphics on walls as high as 30 feet and 100 feet long. One wall is a collage of employee's photos creating a rock concert; another depicts sporting events. They have an indoor basketball goal, scooters, and an employee lounge with a fireplace. It's a fun place to work.

*Relish and share a sense of accomplishment when tasks are completed.*

Take a short break. Go to lunch. Cater lunch. Eat cake. Go buy the beer after work. Have fun. Always congratulate completed tasks regardless how small.

*Create fun competition between teammates and/or teams.*

The key word is "fun." Sometimes even silly challenges can make a dreary day become a fun day. For example, choose one word such as "no" and whoever says "no" the least wins. Competition can be based on performance and production — the most, best, or quickest. It could be who helps others the most; the best new team idea, or even the funniest word of the day.

*Give your team direction*

CAD (commit-assign-deadline) Commit to a goal, assign activities, and set a deadline. Giving direction will make your team more satisfied, especially when they achieve the goal through their plans and you recognize their performance. That's fun.

*Look for fun opportunities*

Celebrate birthdays, employment anniversaries, and holidays. Have a casual dress day, hold a potluck lunch, and ask your team for fun ideas. Embrace fun in the workplace, and you'll be rewarded with happier more productive teammates.

## Should You Be Friends with Direct Reports?

Have you been told not to be friends with your employees? If I asked you, should a boss help his or her direct reports, would your answer be absolutely? However, if you look up the definition of friendship that's what you'll find. Managers are advised not to be friends with employees despite countless examples to the contrary not the least of which is Tony Hsieh, CEO of Zappos, if you haven't read his book Delivering Happiness [deliveringhappinessatwork.com] add it to your shortlist. Not only can you be friends with direct reports — you should be. I think people may be confused by their definition of friendship. Let me explain.

### Friends Don't Encourage Negative Thinking

I've been advised not to be friends with direct reports because, "You'll complain about work to each other." Negativity doesn't help anyone. Complaining to each other doesn't help inside or outside of work. There's no place for complaining about the job or gossiping about other employees in the employee-boss relationship. Offering positive suggestions to improve the workplace — you bet. Indiscriminately griping without offering a solution — not what friends do.

### Friends Do More for Friends

I've been warned, "Employees will take advantage of your friendship." Anyone who takes advantage of another isn't their friend. Friends help each other by learning their needs, wants, and desires. A boss should know what a direct report wants from a job and help them achieve it. When an employee knows the boss has the employee's best interest at heart — they're inclined to give their best. People will go above and beyond to help their friend...even if he or she is the boss. Leader/employee friendships improve performance, reduce turnover, and support a positive work environment.

### Friends are Honest with Each Other

I've been told, "It's hard to hold your friends accountable." Maybe so, but true friends don't lie to each other and the boss/friend can't either. It may not be easy, but as a boss, and friend, you must honestly evaluate performance, give feedback as needed, and hold friends accountable. Don't confuse being nice with being a friend. A friend will help a friend be a better person and employee.

### Friends Know and Observe Boundaries

I've heard, "A boss can't be friends with his team because it's outside of business boundaries." What does that even mean? If I was visiting a friend's family and was told they abhor cursing — I wouldn't curse. It's not much different in the workplace — there are policies to be followed. Romance in the workplace is almost always a mistake and harassment in the guise of friendship isn't friendship...its harassment. Friends respect boundaries.

## One Last Thought About Motivation

It's going to be difficult to motivate others if you're not motivated. Having the desire to help others is a continuous source of motivation. Understanding and embracing the vision of your organization is a source of enthusiasm and pride as well as an effective motivator. Knowing what motivates you and seeking it is important. Determine what gets you excited, energized, and happy — then go for it. There's nothing wrong with letting your boss know what you need. An unhappy manager seldom leads a fun productive team.

Our next step in this journey is conducting employee reviews. Effective, helpful, and honest employee reviews can be a motivator (nice segue huh?)

# Employee Reviews

## Chapter Five

# CHAPTER FIVE: EMPLOYEE REVIEWS

## It's an Ongoing Process

You're responsible for conducting employee reviews for your department, and a direct report's annual or semi-annual review is past due. It's not that you don't want to complete the review — it's because you're so busy and it takes a lot of work to properly prepare for a review. You want to be sure your evaluation is fair and honest. But what message are you sending by being late, especially if salary increases are attached to the review? Sound familiar?

The review process shouldn't be limited to an annual or semi-annual meeting — it should be continuous, ongoing, and constant. If it's been six months or a year since you looked at the previous review, a year since you analyzed improvement areas, a year since you considered the employee's pay structure — then review preparation becomes a time-consuming task. I'm not sure a fair evaluation can be accomplished when it hasn't been looked at for so long. However, if you consider the review a process of improvement to be revisited throughout the year, preparation becomes manageable because you've been preparing all year for the next review.

- **The review process is all year long.** Look at the most recent performance review at least once per month. In other words, review the review. Choose areas where improvement is needed and where improvement has been made and share these with employees throughout the year.

- **Set benchmarks for improvement.** Continuously concentrate on areas of improvement, setting expectations and the activities required to achieve them.

- **Don't surprise anyone.** An employee should have an understanding of their level of performance before the review. If you're interacting and mentoring throughout the year, they'll know where they stand.

### Now You're Ready to Conduct the Review... Almost

- **Come prepared.** Know the positive performance areas and areas that need improvement based on observable behavior, objective criteria, and results.

- **Budget 30–45 minutes.** Give the employee your full attention. Don't allow interruptions.

- **Start with positives.** If you begin with negatives, you take the chance of the employee shutting down. If they've earned a pay increase, that's a positive place to begin — you think?

- **Be honest, but not negative.** Use tact and professionalism; maintain a professional tone, and base critiques on facts.

- **Don't horse around.** An employee review may not be the best time to be glib or joke with the employee.

- **Use activities based performance improvement.** Goals should be activities oriented. Begin with activities to continue, improve, or stop.

What kind of message do you send to an employee when you're late on reviews? If this has happened to you, you already know the answer. The message is you don't care about the employee, you're inconsiderate, and you lack organization.

## Don't Ruin Your Employees

I've run off, hindered, and ruined more direct reports than I want to admit. Too often, when I didn't hold people accountable, I told myself I was a "nice boss." I didn't want the confrontation. That would be unpleasant, and I wanted a pleasant work environment. As long as I viewed it as confrontational, it probably would be, but I began to realize it wasn't confrontational if it came from a desire to help my employee. Have you ever lost an employee you shouldn't have because you were too easy on them? Have you allowed the fear of confrontation to keep you from giving someone the direction he or she needed? Was there more you could've done?

Many potentially productive employees have been hindered or lost by managers who thought they were being "nice." If you want to help, don't ignore areas where improvement is needed, do what needs to be done to help your people develop. If you want to help your subordinates inform them how they're doing — it's not fair if you don't.

Years ago, I told my manager I wanted to fire an employee because they weren't doing their job. My manager listened to me, and then called the employee into the office. He asked the employee how he thought he was doing. The employee felt he was doing a good job, and explained why. After the employee had left the room, my manager looked at me and asked, "How would it be fair to fire anyone who doesn't know they're NOT meeting your expectations?" It was a lesson I've not forgotten.

## Help, Don't Hurt

- Give clear expectations with activities, results, and time frames.

- Inform people when they're not meeting expectations.

- Teach people how to meet expectations.

- Don't go to a third party with a complaint; go to the employee.

- Never delegate without periodically following up on the assignment.

- Review job descriptions.

- Distribute and train written procedures and policies.

- Don't accept sub-standard performance — improve it.

- Offer constant, ongoing training.

It's not complicated, though; at times it does require courage. But remember, it's not confrontation if it's helpful. Do you want to be nice? If so, do what's in the best interest of the employee.

I once had an employee with personal hygiene issues. She worked in a small office — and she smelled bad. It came to my attention when her co-workers came to me and complained. No one had said anything to her, and although her performance was acceptable, they all wanted her fired. I sat down with her privately, explained how the hygiene affected the small work environment, put no blame on her co-workers, and asked if there were any physical problems out of her control. She explained her husband had lost his job, and she didn't want to burden anyone, but they were living out of their car. She agreed to share this with her co-workers, who all offered help. She became one of the hardest working, most loyal employees within the company.

Have the courage to help others reach their potential; don't hinder, hurt, or ruin them by trying to be "nice" as an excuse to ignore the behavior.

## Last Thought

If you embrace the employee review as continuous opportunity to lead improvement, not as a once a year project justifying a team member's pay increase, or lack thereof, you'll find it an indispensable motivating tool. The next chapter is about something that can demotivate and cause problems within your team and also between your team and other departments within your organization. Have you heard of siloing?

# Silo Busting

## Chapter Six

# CHAPTER SIX: SILO BUSTING

## What is a Silo?

Driving through the Midwest, you'll see grain silos standing alone. Each silo is designed for a specific type and amount of grain. Similar to those silos, departments within organizations are designed to accomplish specific tasks. Silo thinking is when a department or a team member stands alone and focus is placed on the individual or department instead of the organization. Often, the department becomes more important to its members than the organization as a whole.

**Have you ever heard, said, or thought the following?**

- It's not my problem.

- They don't work in my department.

- That's what they said to do, so I'm doing it, right or wrong.

- I don't have time to deal with things outside of my team.

If you've observed any of these bullet points in your workplace, you've seen silos in action. Silos are everywhere. They're in every organization and on most teams. Silo thinking destroys teams and undermines organizations. You must constantly uncover, discover, and bust the silos down.

Last year, my father spent two weeks in the hospital and another two weeks receiving daily outpatient treatments. The staff was knowledgeable and treated my father with respect and kindness, unfortunately departments communicated poorly — if at all. Dad was moved to a lesser care unit without the knowledge of his attending physician who moved him back. When I asked how this happened the doctor said, "It doesn't surprise me." My father's treatment dosage was increased after testing, which was done prematurely. The new levels of medication were based on results taken three days before the doctor requested them — before the medication had a chance to stabilize my father. Once again, when I asked how this happened I was answered, "It doesn't surprise me." Near the end of his outpatient treatment, my father and I were asked why we hadn't been there for treatment the previous day. When we said we weren't scheduled the nurse asked if anyone had informed us our treatment schedule had been changed. No. And once again I heard, "It doesn't surprise me." How can service be so poor, possibly life threatening, from so many people who are competent and caring? Because not only do they see their niche as more important than the whole — they'd given up trying to communicate; instead they accepted, "It doesn't surprise me." Although I don't work in health care, I'm not naïve. I understand how immensely difficult coordinating various departments, shifts, and staffs must be, but the answer isn't complacency — don't accept it — don't give up.

Starting something new often exposes silos. In the last few years, I've heard multiple complaints about the difficulty to garner support for social media initiatives. Resistance to change, in this case social media, may be about self-centered turfism — not seeing the big picture and not working for the good of the entire organization. To successfully engage team members in anything, including social media, you have to tear down silos. Sharing the benefits of any new initiative may be the best way to gain acceptance and support. For example, social media can be a marketing tool, PR source, lead generator, customer satisfaction gauge, recruitment tool, and more. Co-workers siloed in one area may not understand the importance of new ideas until it's explained, until the advantages of embracing the initiative are shown — until the silos are gone.

Open your eyes, it's everywhere. I was at a company when a call-to-action television ad aired. The ad produced a high volume of calls for about 15 minutes. The department charged with taking the calls couldn't handle the call volume. Though the department repeatedly asked for help, I observed a dozen people, who had been trained simply to take names and numbers for a call back — not make any effort to help. It wasn't their department. Calls were lost, and potential customers ignored. I imagine some of you reading this are thinking, "I wouldn't have time for that either; it's not my job." If so, take a moment to consider, are you putting your department ahead of the organization?

## Examples of the Silo Effect

### Bureaucratic infighting

Not long ago, there were major fires in a California municipality. Navy helicopters were available and equipped to fight fire. Trained personnel were waiting to respond, however; the trained personnel had not attended the local municipality's fire prevention training and hadn't received local accreditation. They weren't allowed to participate. Thousands of dollars of property were destroyed.

### Self-centered Turfism

Turfism is misplaced loyalty to a department rather than an organization. It's a source of dissension, which hinders performance. While consulting for a company, I observed a shipping manager refuse to ship a parcel that didn't follow standard shipping policy. Rather than fix it, ship it, and work with the department on improving, he held it for a day then sent it back. I asked what he hoped to accomplish and the shipping manager's answer was, "It's the only way they learn." No, it may be one way they learn, among many training options, or they might retaliate. The facts are; the shipping was delayed, customers were put off, and animosity was created within the organization. This example is certainly poor management, which is bolstered by self-centered turfism — the shipping department had become more important than the whole.

During a silo-busting seminar, I asked a group of hard-working managers if they thought they ever exhibited poor work ethic. Then I asked them to consider the following:

Had they ever said, "It's not my job, my department, or my responsibility," Had they ever observed detrimental behavior, procedures not followed, or policies broken, and did nothing because it wasn't their employee? Had they ever advised a team member — capable of helping — let the *other* department handle it? I asked the group to consider how to grade anyone's work ethic if they didn't help the whole team. They were very quiet.

## Causes of Silos

### Poor communication between departments or team members.

When teams understand their roles within the organization, how they interact with other departments, and how they affect each other, they're more inclined to work past silos. Interdepartmental communication and training should include the overall vision of the organization, each department's role, and how they complement and depend on each other. One of the most effective ways to achieve this is by bringing teams together. Shared training, meetings, and seminars help people understand the importance of cooperation.

### Spending more time on planning than working with people.

Planning seldom creates a silo — people do. The best-made plans may be doomed to fail unless people are given interdepartmental expectations and the tools to achieve them.

### Management confusing talks with influence.

It's not too complicated to give a talk, write a memo, send an email with policy or instructions, but will it be followed? Will it be listened to or read? Influence begins with an understanding of what to do, why do it, how to do it, and what it means to the organization. Talk is just that. If you want to make a positive impact, concentrate on what's being done — not what's being talked about. Take action to make traction.

## Silo Busting — How to Tear Down Those Silos

### Cross Training

Some organizations include basic, one-day, interdepartmental cross training as part of new employee orientation. The more understanding of how departments affect each other, the less likely it is to silo. Getting to know the personnel of other departments and their responsibilities helps knock down silos.

### Observation

Shadow employees from other departments; one day of observation could change a year.

### Shared Meetings

Conduct interdepartmental group meetings for recognition, state of the company, vision, or status meetings.

### Seminars

Hold a seminar on team building invite all departments.

### Team Recognition

Look for opportunities to recognize how departments complimented each other.

### Influence the Influencers

You may not have the time or ability to influence everyone, so use the help available to you. Whom does your team look up to? What peers do they hold in high esteem? Determine the influencers and get them on your side by seeking their advice and input. Most people want to make a difference, be part of a team, and know their ideas matter. By opening a dialogue with them you can influence the influencers.

### Go Public

List commitments or post production standings in a public area. For example, TKO Graphix instituted a waste tracking board, by job and department, in a work area seen by most departments. The tracking board helped reduce waste throughout the company, and fostered interdepartmental collaboration. Sharing how each department affected the other in waste management, fostered teamwork. The group had a common goal to reduce waste as a team, which they accomplished.

### Use Ad-hoc Instead of Bureaucracy

Adhocracy is an organization style based on flexibility, unlike the more rigid bureaucracy. As an example, in a bureaucratic manufacturing system a broken machine requires specific channels of communication to be repaired. The repair order would be sent from the machine operator to the supervisor, and then to the supervisor of repair, and finally, to the repair person. This is time-consuming and increases the chance of miscommunication. In the adhocracy, the machine operator would go directly to the repair person.

### Teach Information Gathering and Problem-Solving Techniques

Michael Brown, who headed the Federal Emergency Management Administration when Hurricane Katrina hit New Orleans, had the nearly impossible task of gathering correct information to make informed decisions. As information was processed within FEMA, it was diluted, fitting the realities of various agencies or individuals handling the info — often each relaying what was most significant to their needs, not the whole picture. The bigger the group, the more difficult information gathering becomes; by the time it gets to the war room, the information is often wrong. Decisions made on faulty information usually fail. For example, not sending buses to evacuate the Superdome was based on faulty and diluted information. Before taking action, learn to gather information until you fully understand the situation. If you have ever played the game of telephone, passing a phrase from person to person, you get the idea. Now consider the communication nightmare when information is omitted and edited.

### Apply Activities Management

Although the final results are critical, they're HISTORY. They cannot be changed. Activities are a continuing opportunity to coach, educate, and impact the results — especially when the entire team is involved. Manage the activities, not the results. What activities, affecting the entire company, might be improved, reinstated, added, discontinued, or strengthened?

### Institute Character First

Character First [www.characterfirst.com] is the philosophy of character before ability, skill, or knowledge. Co-workers with strong character traits such as responsibility, self-control, sincerity, thoroughness, and dependability will be less likely to silo — more likely to work as a team.

### Use Many Techniques

Don't rely on one easy answer, one email, one presentation, or a few posters. A single one-hour seminar, alone, will not break the silo. There isn't one easy answer. It requires multiple actions, which are regularly monitored, and repeated. Establish systems, which break silos by fostering teamwork. During a silo-busting seminar, I assigned a group the task of choosing and implementing a silo-busting technique. I provided ideas and examples of silo-busting methods, but told the group they could devise their own. One of the participants outlined a plan to track a customer order from start to finish, recognizing every department's contribution to the completed work. What a great idea! You and your team know best what will work in your business.

In a Newsweek [www.newsweek.com/ciscos-ceo-john-chambers-leadership-73135] interview, Cisco Systems CEO, John Chambers, discussed their leadership's silo-busting plan. "There's a fundamental change that may be really important to the future of business in this country and the world. At Cisco, we are moving to collaboration teams, groups coming together that represent sales, engineering, finance, legal, etc. And we're training leaders to think across silos. We now do that with 70 different teams in the company. So we'll have a sales leader go run engineering. A lawyer go run business development. A business development leader go run our consumer operations. We're going to train a generalist group of leaders who know how to learn and operate in collaboration teamwork. I think that's the future of leadership."

### Don't Point Fingers

One of the greatest enemies of silo busting is finger pointing. Finger pointing and passing the blame, builds silos. Although, at times, most of us point fingers — It's usually more disruptive than helpful. It's easy to do and often seems justified, but even so, what's gained? Regardless of how "real" the blame, blaming will not improve the results; it could make things worse. Without training for improvement, how does attaching blame help? If someone dropped the ball, didn't follow through, or did a poor job — pointing a finger will not make it better (OK, you might feel a little better, but how does that help?) It's not who is right (or wrong) it's what is right. Rather than pointing fingers, concentrate on the activities needed to change the results.

### Stop Griping and Start Helping

- How can you get it done?

- How can you improve it?

- How may it be avoided next time?

- What needs to be changed?

- Who else could help?

Think about it — any excuse becomes a reason not to perform. Do you want to perform at the highest level, or under-perform due to excuses?

# Silo Busting Planner

Choose 1 or 2 activities from the previous list to implement or create your own

_____
_____
_____

Select activity committee members who will help implement these activities

_____        _____
_____        _____
_____        _____
_____        _____

Start date _____

Deadline_____

How will activities be implemented?

_____
_____
_____
_____
_____
_____

How will the activities be monitored and reviewed?

_____
_____

What's in it for the team and individuals?

_____
_____
_____
_____

## An Exercise in Improvement

You're the commander of an army facing horrific conditions — what do you do?

- Most troops lack uniforms, shelter, or warm clothing, including shoes.

- There are severe shortages of food and potable water.

- Over half the troops are sick with dysentery, flu, malnutrition, and worse.

- There is a severe shortage of ammunition.

- Nearly half the citizens of your country are against the war.

- The government is months behind paying your troops.

- You're fighting a highly trained, larger, better-equipped force.

- Volunteers regularly abandon posts — sometimes entire regiments.

History buffs know these are only a few of the obstacles General Washington faced during the American Revolutionary War. I'd say they were substantial roadblocks, but as you know, he didn't use them as excuses. Without going into a history lesson what General Washington did was look for alternatives, find new solutions, think out of the box, and he didn't give up, he didn't make excuses, he didn't silo.

**Quit finger pointing. Stop allowing excuses to affect your performance. Find a way to help.**

## Are you ready to bust some silos?

Common goals help tear down silo walls. When an organization shares a vision and works together, silos are destroyed. One of the most common causes of siloing is a breakdown of communication. Guess what's next?

# Communication

## Chapter Seven

# CHAPTER SEVEN: COMMUNICATION

## Listen First

In management, listening is more important than talking. Often, it's not what you say; it's what you hear that defines communication. Many managers spend time honing presentation skills, but little on improving listening. When direct reports are encouraged to talk, because their manager attentively listens to them, they'll share their needs, wants, and desires — if we listen.

## How to Improve Listening Skills

- **Listen actively by concentrating** on the speaker with the sole purpose of understanding what's being said.

- **Don't interrupt** and don't assume you know what the speaker is going to say — you don't.

- **Keep an open mind** and don't stereotype, prejudge, or assume you know the content before listening. Come to the conversation with an open-mind and a positive attitude.

- **Limit distractions** by giving your full attention to the speaker; turn off your phone and meet in a quiet space. Taking notes and making eye contact may help.

- **Stop thinking about what you want to say.** If you are "waiting" for the speaker to stop so you can get your point across, you're probably not listening. Focus on the speaker.

- **Clarify your understanding** by repeating what you heard such as, "If I understand what you said it was..."

- **Don't take a stance,** listening is not about agreeing or disagreeing; it's about understanding what is being said.

I'm not a good listener, and it has cost me. If there were a poor listener 12-step program, I'd join. Don't misunderstand me — I'm not making light of attentiveness. I realize the importance of listening skills and continue to seek improvement... it's just not natural for me. Is it for you? Are you a good listener?

I sometimes wonder if our loud and fast paced, multi-channel, social media-filled world isn't creating ADHD in all of us. How often do you give only part of your attention to a conversation? When others share their thoughts, are you multi-tasking on your smart phone and checking the score on the big screen while looking at the menu?

On Facebook, I recently asked: "What advice would you offer a new manager that you wish someone had shared with you?" I received enough comments for ten blog posts. This one was from Dawna Clark: "Listen… actively… Stay in check with your personal biases and focal points!"

In the spirit of transparency, I must say my listening skills suck, but I'm working on them. You might ask, "So… why are YOU writing about active listening?" That's easy — I know what NOT to do. I'm constantly working on my listening skills, and the following has been helpful for me.

### Put Your Mind in the Right Place

Whether you're in a conversation or listening to a presentation set the stage by considering what your purpose is. Are you there to learn? Do you want to know what the other person has to share? If you do all the talking, how will this be achieved? You already know what you know. Set your ego aside; this isn't about who's better, bigger, or more knowledgeable — it's not a power struggle (or shouldn't be).

### Who, What, When, and Where

Whenever possible, hold conversations in a quiet place, free of distractions, and put interruptions on hold. Facing one another without obstructions, such as a desk, often leads to more open dialogue.

Avoid emotion. It's not about you. It's about learning what the other person has to share. Be a Vulcan — keep it logical.

Listening has never been easy or simple, but today, it may be more difficult than ever. Developing active listening skills takes hard work, practice, and patience. And in our modern mobile world, it means occasionally unplugging as well. Take the time to listen, make the world a little quieter for a short time — you never know what you might learn.

## How to Improve Communications in 10 Minutes

Poor communication is a problem in every organization. Wouldn't it be worth taking 10 minutes to improve it? From a two-person operation to multinational businesses, poor communication causes delays, overruns, and mistakes. It may be the largest cause of inefficiency in the workplace. There's a solution. It's not complicated, and it's less time consuming than the mistakes caused by poor communication.

### Improving Communication Through Follow up

Regardless of the form — email, texting, social media or verbal — to improve communication, confirm those you've communicated with understand what was said. Here's how:

- **Whenever you can, put it in writing.** The most predictable outcome to verbal communication is misunderstanding. Follow up verbal communication by putting it in an email, text, or memo. Writing helps clarify thoughts and provides a reference.

- **Ask for feedback.** Don't assume your message was properly communicated. It may have been lost, misinterpreted, or ignored. By asking for thoughts, opinions, and suggestions you'll better understand what was gleaned from the initial communication.

- **Confirm what was understood from your communication.** Last year, a manager shared he had communication challenges with most of his team. He wondered if *he* was the problem. I asked if he followed up with his team's understanding of what was said. He replied he did. I asked how? He said, "I always ask, 'do you understand?'" Since most people don't want to appear ignorant or uninformed, many will answer "yes" to this leading question, even if they don't understand. To check understanding, ask people to repeat or explain what's been communicated. For example, "I want to make sure everything's clear. What was my key point as you understood it?"

If you take the time to follow up, confirming your communication, you'll become more effective and efficient at what you do. You'll reduce the time spent fixing poor communication and you can use your time more productively. Does this make sense? It Does? Please share how it makes sense to you? (See what I did?)

# How to Improve Interdepartmental Communication

Communication between divisions and departments is a problem in nearly every type of organization. As important as it is, as many problems as it causes, and as much as everyone wants it improved — little is done in the way of a solution. Improvement comes by understanding the causes and implementing a plan of activities for improvement.

### *Common Causes*
- **Inaccurate and incomplete information** — Not taking the time to check information, sloppy communication, and correspondence delegated to unqualified direct reports may be the underlying issues.

- **Uncommunicated expectations** — If others don't know what is expected, they probably won't meet those expectations. Sounds pretty silly doesn't it? It happens, and it happens often. Don't assume — share.

- **"Yes-man" syndrome** — Someone parroting what others wants to hear, not what's going to occur. Caused by fear of conflict, not wanting to contradict a superior, or worse yet, someone who has no intention of doing anything, unless it's *their* way and doesn't share his or her opinion.

### *Underlying Reasons*

- **Siloing and interdepartmental conflict** — the department becomes greater than the whole.

- **Limited time allotted to communication** — interdepartmental communication not given the importance or time needed.

- **People using different communication media** — I recently had a co-worker upset with me because I hadn't answered their email. I limit the number of times per day I allow email to distract me from tasks, and I expect urgent matters to be delivered via phone — he didn't know that, I hadn't communicated.

- **Assuming others think as we do** — Everyone does this. Miscommunication can be reduced by reviewing the understanding of shared information.

- **Poor listening skills** — see above.

- **Finger pointing** — This seldom improves anything, including communication.

- **Relying on verbal communication alone** — Supplement verbal communication with follow up correspondence.

### *Taking Action to Improve Communication between Departments*

- **Begin the conversation** by conducting periodic leadership seminars involving department heads. Bringing everyone together opens lines of communication.

- **Determine what information is needed** — Facilitate interdepartmental discussions regarding the information needed, what is not being accurately or timely shared, and how to improve this.

- **Talk about how to communicate** — Are interdepartmental expectations to be shared via email, private correspondence, verbally? Who should be copied and when? What is the expected follow up? Ask these questions and share expectations.

- **Cross-train** — Improved understanding, through job rotation of each other's responsibilities and activities, will lead to an appreciation of how departments interact and affect one another, which leads to better communication.

## Last Thought

Is interdepartmental communication a problem in your organization? Has anything been done to improve it? If not, get it started. Begin the conversation, share expectations, learn what others do, and consider how YOU can improve your information sharing.

Our next step is to learn how to set goals that aren't a wish or a hope but concrete activities forming a plan of improvement.

# Goal Setting

## Chapter Eight

# CHAPTER EIGHT: GOAL SETTING

Goals direct an individual or group's behavior. Goals are most effective when they're shared in written statement with clearly described activities and an expected measurable result.

Are you a leader/manager? Do you set and review goals with your team monthly, weekly, daily? If not, why not? If it's because goal setting and review haven't been productive — they can be. If it's because you haven't made time — make it. I've been involved in more corporate team and individual goal setting sessions than I want to remember. Many of them were a waste of time, but a few key factors can make goal setting sessions productive, effective, and efficient.

Goal setting should direct behavior not solely focus on results. To improve results behavior must be modified. Although the goal must focus on measurable objective criteria — results; it's activities that achieve goals. **You can't *do* a goal you have to do activities to reach goals and get results.** Goals should include:

Clearly defined objectives and an activities plan. Over the years, when I've asked team members how they will hit their goals — I've often heard something like:

- I'll do better

- I'll work harder

- I'll do more

The smart aleck in me always wants to ask why they aren't already working harder, doing better, or doing more. Don't accept these non-specific generalized answers. Follow up with open-ended questions such as:

- What will you do better?

- How will you do it?

- When will you begin?

- How will you work harder?

**You Cannot Do a Goal. You Can Only Do Activities!** Goals not coupled with activities to reach them are meaningless and futile. Goals without a plan to achieve them are only wishes. Although degree of difficulty, time limits, measurability, conditions, objective criteria, etc., should be discussed — it will be difficult to achieve any goal without a clear plan of activities.

## Plan the Activities

- What activities should be repeated?

- What activities need improved?

- What needs to be discontinued?

- Where is help needed?

- What activities need changed?

- What activities should be renewed? (successful activities previously performed)

When I was in a position of managing managers, I asked a young team leader how the previous month's goals had progressed. In great detail, he enthusiastically showed me his team's improvements. He explained the activities, which helped them improve, and since they had financial incentives, he also bragged about their financial gains. After congratulating him and the team, I asked about the current month's goals (we were four or five days into the new month). The team leader had not "got to it." He didn't follow up and repeat the goal setting activity that had helped his team meet their goals the previous month. The point is — don't get away from activities that work. The most important activity may be defining, analyzing, and setting...activities. When you set goals with activities, you may discuss activities every day — not only the results. As I've mentioned twice previously (not six times yet) we may learn from results, but they're history, we must know what activities caused the results if we wish to improve or repeat the outcome.

After reading this a friend told me, "I really don't care about activities unless they produce concrete results." Here's my answer. It takes activities to achieve results. Only by analyzing those activities can results be modified. Without a set of activities to follow we only hope to get results. If we want to maintain or improve results we must know what activities affect the outcome and how, then plan accordingly.

## Leaders Improve Those Around Them

If you're in a leadership position, you're expected to improve your team. This is accomplished both as a group and on an individual basis. As leaders, we should ask ourselves daily:

- What have I done to improve the team today?

- Would the team have done as well without me today?

Improvement can begin with effective goal setting. To set a goal, you must analyze what activities impact the goal and follow up.

# 6 Ingredients of a Goal

1. **Difficulty: The goal must be challenging, yet not impossible.**
   A team member I once worked with proudly showed me his previous month's goals. He had listed goals and activities on a sheet. He had stuck with his goals even though his team leader had crossed off the individual monthly production goals as unrealistic. He beat the original crossed out production goal by 10 percent. The moral here is to be careful not to clip a team member's wings by limiting achievable expectations. If they believe it can be achieved, have a plan of activities to reach the goal, and it's possible to achieve, support them.

2. **Measurable: Base goals on measurable performance to avoid vague goals.**
   Goals must be based on objective criteria, for example, statistics, which can be compared, tracked, and paced. I have hit and surpassed more individual and team goals by pacing and adjusting goals than any other activity. To pace a goal:

   - Take the results-to-date; for example, you've sold ten items

   - Divided the results by a unit of time (hour, day, week, or month) You've sold ten items in five days = Two sold per day

   - Multiply that by the unit of time for the entire goal — Let's say 30 days, so 30 days X two per day = a pace of 60 items to be sold.

   Here's another example, let's say the goal for a team member was to produce 300 widgets in a month (21 working days).

   - Five days into the goal, 60 widgets were completed; 60 widgets divided by five days =12 widgets produced per day.

   - Now, take the average 12 widgets produced per day, times 21 workdays, and the sum is 252, which is 48 widgets short of the goal.

   - With 16 days remaining, how many widgets, per day, will need to be made to hit 300?

- Subtract the 60 widgets made from the 300 goal = 240 divided by 16 remaining days. The answer is 15 per day to hit the goal of 300.

In the example above — adjustments can be made to hit the goal. Pacing measures progress towards a goal and allows for adjustments. Without knowing where you are on a goal the result is always a surprise. Was that something Yogi Berra said?

3. **Activity Driven: Positively reinforce or modify behavior by specifying activities and how they will be modified.**
Although every part of the goal is important, activities are the most important. Consider what activities should be continued, stopped, improved, resumed, or need help.

4. **Time Limits: Set start dates, periods to review progress, and an end date.**
Review the goals throughout the period. That way, you may modify activities and behavior to help reach the goal.

5. **Consider aiding or hindering conditions.**
Aiding conditions such as a windfall contract, early supply delivery, or unexpected vendor price reductions may be cause to adjust (increase) a goal accordingly. Hindering conditions like economic upheaval, technological obsolescence, and an evolving marketplace may indicate the need for goal reduction — but not always. The best example I can recall of overcoming hindering conditions was a retail organization's goal. The East Coast-based B2C set a goal to beat its all-time one-month volume record. Unfortunately, the month they picked also happened to be the month the stock market plunged, banks failed, and in general, the nation experienced an economic downturn. Undaunted, they redoubled their efforts, reworked their plans, and beat the record. That's leadership.

6. **Rewards: Reinforce the behavior and activities.**
Often, when I mention rewards, people assume I mean financial rewards — maybe, maybe not. What motivates the team or the team member? A reward could be recognition, time off, or other enticements.

**Where do you begin?** Gather previous objective results — objective results may include standards, benchmarks, results, and numbers. It should not include subjective opinions. Use the following list to be certain you're ready before setting goals.

**Goal Checklist:**

- Clear, trackable objectives.

- Clearly defined activities.

- Measurable result.

- Time limits.

- Challenging, but not impossible.

- Conditions, both aiding and hindering, are considered.

# Example Goal Setting Form

Team Member: _____ Today's Date: _____ Goal Begins: _____

Review Dates: _____ _____ _____ _____ Ends: _____

Objective Criteria and Previous Results Goal

_____

Activities to continue

_____

_____

Activities to stop

_____

_____

Activities to improve

_____

_____

Activities to add

_____

_____

Other activities

_____

_____

Aiding and/or hindering conditions

_____

_____

Team member x_____Date_____

# How to Use the Goal Setting Form

- Complete the objective criteria and previous results boxes.

- Analyze, through observable behavior, activities that will influence the outcome; however, don't complete the section at this time.

- Calculate realistic objective improvements, but don't fill in the goal box.

- Set a period to begin, review, and end the goal.

- Set a time to review the goal privately with each team member.

- Ask the team member for their realistic goals for each objective. If it's unrealistic, direct them to a more realistic goal.

- Review each activity category and ask the team member what activities they will complete to hit the goal. They don't have to have an action for every activity listed; however, you may direct them in any activity you deem necessary. Clearly define the activities with action verbs, such as, increase, decrease, add, stop, create, organize, improve, design, etc.

### How to Follow Up Goals Daily

Let's say 14.3 widgets are needed per day, or 1.78 per hour, to reach the goal of 300 for the month. Is it being done? If so, what activities can be repeated? If not, what activities need to be adjusted?

- How are procedures being followed?

- What behaviors should be reinforced, or what activities need adjusting?

- How productive are systems and processes?

- How goal focused is the team member?

- How has the goal and activities been communicated?

- Where is help needed, with who, about what, when, how, and why?

- What conditions hinder the results such as, in the case of widgets a parts shortage? If so, does the goal need adjusted?

Keep in mind; it's the team member's goal, not yours. Have them complete the activities section of the goal form. They should embrace the goals as their own. With this in mind, the more they participate in goal setting, and the less you control it, the better.

Regardless of how you define success, use objective criteria to track goals. If your success isn't measured by production, how is it measured? Customer satisfaction, referrals, limiting mistakes, meeting deadlines, or? Is it measured by number of words written, graphics designed, or new employees hired? Whatever the metric used to measure your success some form can be quantified and tracked. How is your success measured?

### What to do AFTER the Goal is Set

Start by supporting, encouraging, and reviewing the goal every day. I remember a team member who missed a quarterly financial reward by a very small amount. It wouldn't have taken much extra effort to hit the bonus — a few more sales calls or one extra evening of work probably would've been sufficient. The team manager didn't know how close his direct report was to achieving the bonus until it was too late. I asked the manager what he thought about his team member missing the bonus by so little and he said, "The employee should have known where he stood." I agreed, and asked him whose responsibility it was to keep the employee informed. He answered, "It was the employee's responsibility." I followed by asking, "If this was the case...why did he need a manager?" One of a manager's responsibilities is to motivate his or her team. The bonus was a tool to motivate team members to excel. If as managers, we don't use the motivating tools, available to us, to help our team achieve higher levels of performance those same tools become demotivating.

*How to Help Your Team Hit Their Goals*

- Talk about what it will do for them and the team.

- Encourage them to go public with the goal, share it with other team members, friends, and family.

- If needed, break the goal into smaller steps with deadlines.

- Keep them focused on activities, not only the results.

- Remind, review, or support their goals in some fashion daily.

- Track and pace the goal, adjusting activities to meet the goal.

- Discuss the goal with them, assume they will achieve the goal, and support them at every opportunity.

- Recognize progress with their peers present, and reward them for their accomplishments.

If you take nothing else from this chapter, take this — focus on activities and follow up.

## Last Thought

If you've taken the time to set an achievable, yet challenging, goal based on activities take the time to review and follow up daily. It will make your job easier. Activities make an impact while focusing on the results usually doesn't change anything. Results can only be improved through activities. Activities are the roadmap to success. Be the map.

# Behavior Modification

# CHAPTER NINE: BEHAVIOR MODIFICATION

Modifying behavior to improve performance is part of a leader's report card. Your direct reports should do better because of your actions and influence, not despite your influence.

## Six Steps to Changing Behavior

Most people will continue to act as they always have. Often, behavior must be changed before improvement can be made. Leaders often become frustrated because logical, common sense solutions don't always bring a change.

I've used the following six-step behavior modification plan with many leadership development trainees. As part of the training, trainees were required to make a six-step plan to modify one of their own behaviors. It could be a personal or work-related behavior they wished to modify. Whether it was going to the gym twice per week and using the membership they bought last year, cutting back on fast food, or improving time management, **the point was** to understand how behavior could be modified regardless of whether it was work specific. Once completed the majority realized success and modified their behavior.

For a behavior to change, it must be observed. It's difficult to change a team member's attitude — meaning, how they feel or what they think. For example, changing an employee with a "bad attitude" is difficult, if not impossible, if we only focus on the employee's mindset. However, if behaviors such as being impolite to other employees, curt on the phone, or rude to customers are observed, they can be modified.

The example of a non-specific behavior, a bad attitude, isn't only too general to be of use — it's often misunderstood. Don't confuse passion with negativity. Is it negative if a teammate insists on procedures being followed? How about pushing everyone on the team to hit quotas? Is bringing detrimental behavior to leadership's attention negative? The obvious answer is a resounding no; however, I've watched leadership (or lack thereof) approaching all these scenarios as negative coming from "bad" employees. It's not negative to follow procedures, and policies. It's not negative to desire to improve the team. Negativity is the opposite. It's when team members complain, become disgruntled, and undermine the procedures, policies, culture, and leadership of the organization. Thank you for indulging me. That's enough of that rant, back to B-mod (behavioral modification.)

## Six-Step Behavior Modification Plan

### 1. Define the Behavior Based on Specific Observable Behavior

Unacceptable: A non-specific definition: "He or she has a bad attitude."

Acceptable: A specific definition could include:

- He or she openly complains about other employees, customers, and the organization.

- He or she submits incomplete, inaccurate work.

- He or she resists following procedures, policies, and systems.

- He or she defies the management.

## 2. Set the Objective to Increase or Decrease the Behavior

Think small; a slight increase or decrease is a modification. Attempting to modify multiple observable behaviors at one time or expecting drastic improvement in a short time will most likely not produce the desired results. Begin with small steps. Make one change at a time.

## 3. Consequences

- Positive reinforcement — rewards for behavioral changes

- Negative reinforcement — reprimand for not changing behaviors

- Extinguish or ignore — no outcome

Before assigning consequences consider the following:

- **Why is the behavior allowed?** Most reoccurring behaviors are reinforced. What is reinforcing the behavior?

- **How is the behavior reinforced?** To understand what's reinforcing the behavior, observe what happens before, during, and after the behavior. Is it ignored, allowed, given exception?

- **If a reprimand has been used, why hasn't it worked?** It may be split reinforcement, which is when a team member likes to "stir things up." What might seem to be a punishment such as a reprimand may reinforce the behavior for those who relish attention. Consider using extinction (ignoring the behavior) to stop split reinforcement.

- **What consequences may not change the behavior?** If your first reaction is creating fear, you might reconsider. In most cases, management through fear should be the last resort. Fear may cause an opposite negative effect, and the more it is used, the less effective it is. Using fear as a motivator is unsustainable and more often than not — counterproductive.

- **When should positive behavior be rewarded?** Whenever it's earned and as soon as possible. Reinforcement can be social (ex: praise), tangible (ex: extra break or time off), or monetary (ex: a bonus).

- **What consequences may be used?** Consequences should adhere to company policy, meet all compliances, and be possible.

## 4. Implement the Plan

- Be consistent — don't praise one day and not the next, or extinguish one time, then through frustration, lash out the next day. Consistently praise positive behavior.

- Combine consequences — the three points listed below, when used together, are an example of combined consequences. In this case for a team member that uses negativity to gain attention.

  - Inform the team to ignore insignificant negative comments.

  - Give a written reprimand to extremely negative, inappropriate behavior.

  - Reinforce all positive behavior immediately.

## 5. Track the Plan

- Can the action be tracked? We control what we track. If it can't be tracked, it can't be modified. Find the objective criteria behind the actions you wish to change.

- Can it be observed? To be tracked, it must be observable behavior or objective criteria. As in tracking, if it can't be observed, documented, or counted...it will be difficult to alter. For example, if someone says he or she wants to "do better" first they need to know what they've been doing, how they've been doing it, and what activities they plan to change to do better.

- How will it be tracked?

- When will it be tracked?

- Who will track it?

- How long will it be tracked?

## 6. Evaluate the Plan before Beginning

- Is it a specific observable behavior?

- Does the plan keep adjustments small, concentrating on one change at a time?

- Can the behavior be tracked?

- Do you know what is reinforcing and controlling the behavior?

- Are the consequences feasible to implement?

- Will this plan be consistent?

Remember, for the six step behavior modification plan to work it must be observable and trackable. Keep it simple. Wouldn't you be encouraged by modifying one team member's behavior every week regardless of how small? Here are some examples of simple, observable, and trackable behavior modification programs:

### Example 1

1. **Observe the behavior.** The team member says negative statements after taking phone calls from difficult customers, which creates a negative environment in the department. Help the team member by defining negative comments.

2. **Set the objective.** To reduce negative comments

3. **State the consequences.** After a week of tracking if the number of negative comments decreases the teammate is rewarded with a suitable reward for example, lunch with the boss (that is if he or she enjoys the bosses company.)

4. **Implement** the plan. The team leader will review the results daily for a week.

5. **Track the Plan.** The team member will use a legal pad, calendar, or spreadsheet to record every instance of a negative comment, totaling the number daily — it doesn't have to be pretty, just accurate.

6. **Review.** Is this plan based on observable behavior, is it trackable, and does it use simple effective consequences?

*Example 2*

1. **Observe the behavior.** Although the company has access to exercise facilities and the teammate previously took advantage of them, they've stopped using the gym, and have expressed a desire to restart.

2. **Set the objective.** To restart using the exercise facilities.

3. **State the consequences.** Every time the teammate works out they receive a voucher and after a period of time they receive a gift certificate for work out apparel.

4. **Implement the plan.** The leader will follow up weekly.

5. **Track the plan.** The team member is to track the vouchers on a calendar, chart, or graph.

6. **Review the plan.**

# Don't reinforce "bad" behavior

What message do you send when you allow poor behavior? Accepting behavior detrimental to the organization, team, or goals reinforces it. It's not going away unless something is done. Don't accept it — change it. Unwarranted exceptions reinforce negatively behavior. The exception becomes the rule, justifying any exception to policy and standards, even as a one-time event moves the bar — precedent has been set for future reference. Not only has the exception become the new rule, but also when many exceptions are made this becomes a general policy. In other words, every policy and procedure becomes exceptionable.

## Six-Step Behavior Modification Outline

1. **Is it based on observable behavior?** Describe the observable behavior to be modified in the simplest terms possible.

   _____
   _____
   _____

2. **Set the objective** — To increase or decrease the observable behavior.

   _____
   _____
   _____

3. **Consider consequences** — List positive, negative, no outcome, or combinations of consequences.

_____

_____

_____

4. **Implement** — When will the plan begin and end? How and when will the plan be followed up?

_____

_____

_____

5. **Track the plan** — Is it observable, simple, trackable? Who will track the plan, and how will it be tracked.

_____

_____

_____

6. **Evaluate the plan** — Review the entire plan.

_____

_____

_____

## One Last Thought — Be the First

Before you run out and start behavior modifications on your teammates — try it on yourself. Create a six step B-mod plan, invest a week, and work on modifying your own behavior. It doesn't matter if it's a work related or personal modification — either will show you how it works. Keep it simple, track it, and follow through with consequences.

Next up we tackle the ugly problem of conflict management. Every team will experience conflict and conflict between departments is common. Nothing can tear down a team faster than festering unrelieved conflict. Knowing how to manage conflict is key to team building.

# Conflict Management

# CHAPTER TEN: CONFLICT MANAGEMENT

In any group of people, there will be disagreements and misunderstandings, which can lead to conflict. Unresolved conflict reduces production, lowers performance, and fosters resentment. In the past you may have stayed above the fray, avoided conflict, or you may have been part of it, but now it's your responsibility to manage it.

## The Pinch Theory of Conflict Management

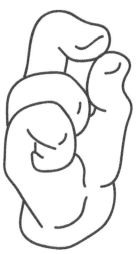

The pinch theory is based on the idea that conflict can be predicted and reduced. When expectations between people are not met, a *pinch,* or a breakdown in the existing relationship, is created. Pinches are inevitable, but can be reduced and managed. A pinch is anything that adversely affects your working relationship with a team member. It may be work related, for example, a difference in procedures that you don't understand or agree with. It could be the work environment such as co-worker's music. Or it could be a communication breakdown.

- Sharing expectations reduces pinches.

- Understanding others personalities minimizes pinches.

- Discussing pinches as soon as they occur avoids escalation and reduces stress.

When pinches are unresolved, allowed to fester, they lead to a *CRUNCH* — defined as an intolerable pinch.

### How do we try to un-crunch?
If you've tried these strategies, you know how poorly they work.

- Ignore the pinch, maybe it will go away.

- Shake hands and make up without resolution. If nothing has changed, nothing will change.

- Avoid conflict by limiting contact. Shunning co-workers doesn't track well in the work place, but how many of you reading this have done just that?

Or you could...

### Agree to Form a Plan to Avoid Pinches
1. **Introduce the pinch.** Here are a few examples.

- "There's something on my mind I need your help understanding."

- "I'm bothered by something — and if I don't tell you what I'm thinking, it's not fair to you or me."

- "Could you spare a minute to talk about something that is bothering me?"

- "I want to talk about something I'm concerned could affect our work together if I don't share it."

2. **Describe the behavior in observable terms**. Do not be accusatory, blame oriented, or confrontational.

   - "Did I hear correctly when you said___?

   - What were you trying to accomplish when you said/did _____?

3. **Describe how you were affected. Own the emotions.**

   - "When you (observable behavior) I felt/thought _____. If I may ask, what was your reasoning?"

   - "When you said _____, I took it to mean _____. How did you intend it?"

   - "I'm not sure I'm clear about _____ would you mind explaining?"

4. **Share your solution**

   - "If you're going to _____ I'd like to understand why/when."

   - "I'd prefer if you would keep me in the loop, please."

   - "Would you mind going over that with me before you do it again?

5. **Come to an understanding.** Let the other party discuss their thoughts, wants, and feelings as early in the conversation as possible. Forge a mutual agreement on how you both intend to respond in the future.

   - "I'd like to create a plan to avoid this. How do you think this can be accomplished?"

   - "What do you think we can do to improve our communication?"

If I visited your workplace, and someone said, "Look at that old white haired man," which should I do? (By the way, my hair is light blonde...very light blonde.)

- Go to a third party and express my dislike.

- Show anger toward the commentator.

- Retaliate by finding something I dislike about them and sharing it.

- Calmly discuss with the commentator my dislike.

Seems pretty silly doesn't it, but have you ever done any of the first three, I have?

## Pinch Meeting Procedure

- Put your thoughts in writing before the meeting.

- Meet in a private room without interruption.

- Turn off your phones.

- Communicate respectfully with understanding.

- Don't allow it to be angry, emotional, or petty. Treat each other with courtesy.

- Listen attentively.

- Forge an agreement, an understanding.

- Honor the agreement.

- Don't share the agreement with anyone else.

The majority of pinches should be resolved at this time, however, if a resolution is not completed, a facilitator might be needed for a second meeting.

# Pinch Meeting Form

1. **The pinch** - Share the action, the pinch. "There's something on my mind I need your help understanding."

_____

_____

_____

2. **Share your view, not the blame** "I feel/think/believe..."

_____

_____

_____

3. **Forge an agreement** "I'd like to form a plan to avoid this. How do you think this can be accomplished?"

_____

_____

_____

_____

Team member agreement

x _____ Date _____

x _____ Date _____

This agreement is only for the teammates involved.

It is not to be shared with other parties.

At one time, I was the most accessible senior manager to more than 100 employees. I spent much of my time resolving conflicts. I'd always considered myself someone who wanted to help others, but this wasn't the help I imagined sharing. I wanted to help people with work skills, character development, and leadership training. I wanted to teach, train, and educate. Resolving the conflict of one employee eating another's snacks didn't fit my definition of education. The pinch theory was introduced and incorporated. It was added to the policy book, presented in new hire orientation, and explained in sub-group meetings. My time spent managing conflict was drastically reduced.

# Corrective Action

Corrective action should never be avoided for fear of confrontation. By using a plan of action, procedures, expectations, and consequences to improve performance, corrective action becomes a tool to help, not to confront.

If we define corrective action as procedures established to modify behavior — a plan of activities, expectations, and consequences to improve performance, then corrective action becomes help.

Too often "corrective action" (disciplinary action) is defined as a process to improve below-standard performance. It should be viewed as a method to change activities, which have the best chance to improve performance. Don't base disciplinary action on performance alone. As much as results are important, telling someone they must do more or better without knowing WHY they aren't doing more or better, WHAT they need to do, and HOW to do it — is seldom productive.

To affect improvement you must answer:

- What behaviors are causing the low performance?

- How behaviors can be positively modified?

- What activities will modify the behavior?

**When is corrective action appropriate?**

Sometimes managers become confused as to when to use disciplinary action — it should be required when team members have **decided** not to follow procedures or policies. Before administering disciplinary action consider the following.

- Were expectations given, are procedures in place?

- Has the team member been competently trained, understands, and is able to use the procedure?

- Were there consequences outside of the team member's control that affected the performance or outcome?

If a team member was trained and unhindered by outside consequences, then they've **decided** not to follow a procedure. In other words, when a team member knowingly and willfully breaks or ignores policies or procedures, they have decided to break the rules. Any and every time a team member decides not to follow a procedure, disciplinary action is not only appropriate — it's required.

Corrective action forms should include:

- Type of action - verbal, written, or disciplinary.

- Reason for the action.

- Corrective action to be taken by the employee.

- Consequences of not adhering to the corrective action.

## How to Complete a Corrective Action Form

- Meet privately with the team member. You may consider another supervisor as a witness depending on the severity of the infraction and/or the personality of the team member.

- Explain to the team member that the ultimate goal of the meeting is to help.

- Explain the type of action. For years, many organizations have used an arbitrary three-strike rule. If the severity of the disciplined action isn't taken into consideration one of two things may occur — unwarranted termination or if an exception is made general disbelief in the three strike system. The type of action should be equal to the degree of the infraction. A minor infraction may be addressed as a verbal warning and a disciplinary action may be the first action if warranted.

  **Verbal** — This is often used as a first warning. If the behavior continues, it may proceed to a written warning or another verbal may be used depending on the severity of the action. It may be best to document this action as a reminder.

  **Written** — Don't sugar coat the warning, if the consequences may include termination, then tell it like it is.

**Disciplinary suspension or termination** — Before completing a disciplinary suspension consider the following: has the team member been given the training, support, and opportunity to succeed? Were there clear expectations, specific actions, trained competencies, and all within the team member's control?

- Clearly and succinctly explain the reason for the action. The reason could include incidents, witnesses, dates, circumstances, and others involved. The reason should not be performance alone. If it is due to poor performance — base it on the activities that caused the sub-standard performance. In this way, the leader and team member have areas to concentrate on to improve the performance.

- The corrective action should include the activities expected of the team member — what, when, and how.

- The consequences are what the team member can expect from management if they don't follow the corrective action. The consequences should be clear, concise, and specific.

- Ask the team member if they are clear about the reason for the corrective action, actions expected, and the consequences. Have the team member sign and date the form.

**What if an employee refuses to sign a corrective action?**

Before asking an employee to sign a corrective action, ask them to put their "side of the story" in comments. Whether they agree with the action or not, the important point, for them, is to document their view. In most cases, when it's explained like this, people are more willing to sign the document, verifying their comments.

# The Sandwich Method

The sandwich is a method of one-on-one critique. The purpose of using the sandwich is to give constructive criticism without causing the **employee to become defensive, angry or close-minded**. When I was introduced to this method years ago, I considered it some sort of trick to be used against employees but It's not, if it's used correctly — and it's honest.

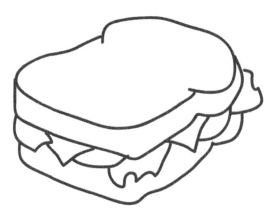

You begin by sharing what you respect about the team member. It has to be real or don't use it. **The first slice of bread** should be a character trait you truly appreciate about the person. It could be their dependability, hard work, dedication, enthusiasm, or diligence. What if there's nothing you appreciate about the individual? You may not know them well enough to complete the critique, so consider spending time to get to know them or ask a manager who does know them to complete the critique. **The meat is the critique.** The critique should be specific. It should be about observable behavior not about personality and never attack-oriented or fear-based. It should include what is expected and how to accomplish this. It also should include a commitment from the employee to change their behavior. **The bottom slice of bread** should again be something you appreciate about the employee or as simple as asking them if they know why you are "going over" this with them. Their answer should be to help them. The sandwich method is one of the most effective management tools you can add to your tool box. To learn more view the three-minute video "How to Critique Without Creating Animosity" [www.youtube.com/watch?v=2IfMMsfp2P8].

## Help Form

A young manager came to me and asked, "How can I make a corrective action non-confrontational?" I explained it should never be confrontational. Conducting a corrective action should come from an attitude of help; corrective actions should be based on facts and presented in a non-condescending, non-accusatory, non-threatening way. The young manager then said, "Well, could we call it a help form?" Other than your organization's HR procedures disallowing an additional form, why couldn't a help form be used?

# Help Form

Coach (Print) _____

Team Member (Sign) X_____
Date_____

**Focus (What needs changed?)**

_____
_____
_____
_____

**Expectations**

_____
_____
_____
_____

**Actions**

_____
_____
_____
_____

**Consequences**

_____
_____
_____
_____

**Comments**

_____
_____
_____
_____

# Sample Corrective Action Form

Name _____ Date _____

Manager _____ Date _____

Type of action    Verbal _____ Written _____ Disciplinary _____

**Reason for the action** (include procedures not followed, dates, circumstances, and others involved):

_____
_____
_____

**Employee will take the following corrective action** (*Activities to be changed*):

_____
_____
_____

**Consequences of not following the corrective action:**

_____
_____
_____

**Employee comments:**

_____
_____
_____
_____

Employee x_____ Date _____

Manager  x_____ Date _____

## The Last Word on Conflict Management

Conflict can't be eliminated, however it can be reduced. First, by recognizing pinches and managing crunches, and secondly, by avoiding conflict created by poorly administered corrective actions. Anytime a group of people interact on a continuing basis there will be misunderstandings, poor communications, and unmet expectations. If you teach your team to be aware of the indicators, then through your guidance, follow through, and positive reinforcement, conflict can be managed. Conflict management isn't the only problem you'll face. I can't predict what problems lie ahead for you. You should expect personnel, performance, and production problems. What I CAN share are a few simple problem solving methods.

# Problem Solving

## Chapter Eleven

# CHAPTER ELEVEN: PROBLEM SOLVING

A decision needs to be made. It's your call. What do you do? Consult your Ouija board, throw darts, or use structured techniques to analyze the situation and plan activities, which lead to a possible solution? It's a leader's responsibility to direct problem solving, not bury his or her head in the sand and hope problems go away. Offering direction through decision-making is a leader's job.

# 7 Steps to Problem Solving

It's easy to get lost in a problem. How do you know where to begin? The answer is, you won't always know. Problems come in all sizes and shapes. The seven-point plan below walks through the key elements of problem solving. It may or may not take all seven steps to realize a solution.

1. **Define the Solved State** — Begin by considering the outcome you desire. Describe the problem when it's no longer a problem. What does it look like?

   - What do you want to achieve?

   - What do you want to eliminate?

   - What do you want to keep?

   - What do you want to avoid?

2. **Determine the Causes** — To define the problem, you must understand the causes. Ask yourself and others the questions outlined below. Gather information and input.

   - What is observable?

   - What objective criteria can be measured?

   - When and where is the problem?

   - What employees, departments, tools, systems, equipment, etc. are involved?

     **Caution:** don't get caught up in the "blame game." Often, the first reaction to a problem is finding someone to blame rather than defining the problem and causes. Blaming others will not solve the problem and is seldom an effective problem solving strategy.

3. **Define the Problem** — Use the solved state and the causes to define the problem. Combining numbers one and two may give you additional insights.

- When does the problem occur?

- How would you describe the problem?

- How can the problem be isolated?

- What sets the problem apart?

4. **Diagram the Problem** — It doesn't have to be pretty. Take the information you have gathered, including the solved state, causes, positions, departments, systems, equipment, tools, etc., and diagram the problem. For some, not all, seeing the problem diagramed offers opportunities for improvement. Here's an example of a process diagram. Diagramming the process may show how parts connect (or don't) and possible areas for improvement.

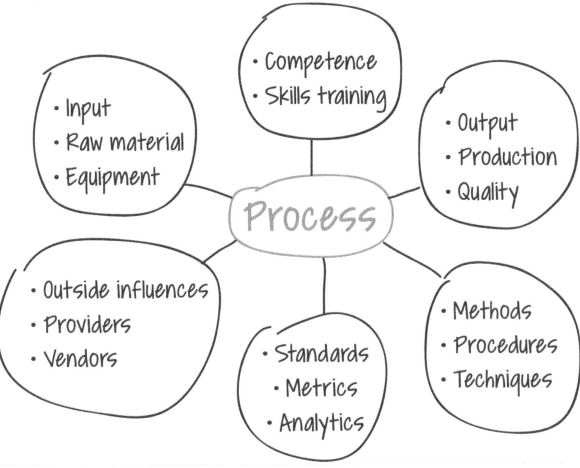

5. **Develop Solutions** — Consider the following points when constructing a solution:

- If the problem is complex, it may be best to break it into parts

- Keep in mind something can be done. Don't accept a problem as unsolvable and remember not every solution will work. Consider looking at the problem as an opportunity to improve.

- Analyze. Does the solution take you to the solved state? If the solved state is clear, but the problem is hard to define, begin at the solved state and go back. For example, if the solved state is consistently producing blog content it might flow as follow:

    a. Solved state = five posts every week.

    b. Schedule set times to write.

    c. Write posts ahead of schedule

    d. Create an editorial calendar.

- People work harder implementing their own plans. Involve everyone, as much as possible, in the planning.

- Solve the problem that exists, not the one you hope exists. Don't guess the cause of the problem or jump to conclusions. Don't try to solve a problem that doesn't exist because it's the problem you know how to solve. Too often we look for the problem we want — not the problem that is.

6. **Implement the Plan — Don't wait. Start solving the problem.**

- When will it begin and end? Set the start time and a deadline.

- Who will lead the solution team?

- How will progress be tracked?

- How will you know the problem is solved?

7. **Review the Progress**

- Is the plan realistic?

- Is the plan on-schedule?

- Does the plan need improvements, additions?

- When will you meet with the team to analyze the results of the plan

# Problem Solving Outline

Name _____Date _____

Describe the solved state

_____
_____
_____

Define the problem

_____
_____
_____

Diagram the problem (use a separate sheet as needed)

_____
_____
_____

Outline the solution

_____
_____
_____

Plan the Implementation of the solution

_____

_____

_____

Schedule follow up

_____

_____

_____

# Specific Problem-Solving Techniques

There is no one-size-fits-all solution to your problems — the following are suggestions to help focus you and your team on solutions.

### Brainstorming

- **Freely share ideas.** In a brainstorming session, there should be no judgment or criticism of ideas. This inhibits sharing. You should encourage everyone to share any and all ideas, however, outlandish or far-fetched.

- **Solicit contributions from everyone**. The more ideas, the better. One idea may spur 10 others.

- **List ideas**. When complete, have the group pick the top ideas, then select which ideas you plan to implement.

### Internalizing

In many ways this process is the polar opposite of brainstorming, but may be appropriate when problem solving sensitive subjects, personnel issues, or when brainstorming has proven ineffective.

Robert Dillon, president of Unique Home Solutions, calls this exercise internalization. He gathers as much information as he can, then thoroughly considers the information before making a decision. Gather information, get the facts, and don't rush. Take the time you need to make your best decision. Remain objective. Don't make a decision without the facts. No matter how urgent the problem, snap decisions may cause bigger problems. Take a deep breath and gather information. Too often, managers rush to decisions based on limited or incorrect information.

# How to Internalize your Way to a Solution

**Internalizing: Procedure Exists**

Is there an existing system, guidelines, or standard operating procedure to cover this instance?

Are all team members involved and informed about the procedure? If not, train them.

Were there consequences out of the team's control, preventing them from using the procedure? Can the consequences be controlled? If so, how?

Was the team informed about the procedure, yet they decided not to follow it? If so, corrective action should be considered.

**Internalizing: No Procedure**

Was this a non-repeating, rare occurrence, which does not require a procedure? You may consider training to empower employees to cope with similar scenarios.

Was this a concern that will reoccur and requires a procedure? Ask the team to help develop the system.

Do you currently have a procedure that does not adequately cover the occurrence? Have the team reevaluate or update the current system

Evaluate the process. What commitments did you receive? What was learned? How can you improve your part in the process?

**Follow up**

Is the new procedure being used?

Does it work, and is it realistic?

Does it need adjusted or improved?

When problems are about sensitive issues people may hesitate to give input in a group. Conducting individual information gathering sessions in private may be more productive. Don't discuss the concern in the hallway, the workspace, or anywhere the conversation may be inappropriate to share.

### Visualization

- Imagine you're working in the department or position where the problem occurs. What happens? Why is it happening? What would you change?

- Picture the solution. How does the solved state operate? Imagine every aspect of the solved state, and play it out.

### Modeling

Modeling the problem may offer insights not apparent in more traditional problem solving methods. For example, if I model the problem of inconsistent blog posting as a recipe — I can see the ingredients of scheduling with an editorial calendar and making time to write as integral parts of the recipe and how, similar to baking a cake, leaving out an ingredient affects the outcome.

- **Construction Model:** Build the solution one phase at a time from the ground up. What are the foundation, the walls, the roof, and the interior?

- **Recipe Model:** What are the ingredients, proportions, spices, cooking time?

- **Automobile Model:** What are the primary systems of a car — engine, transmission, and body? Or it can be taken further into components of the systems such as the engine has spark plugs, oil, coolant, and fuel. How is the problem like these systems and components?

My wife recently experienced a situation where a plan, which she took part in creating, was changed without her consultation. The result was confusion and adoption of two separate plans. Once a plan has been submitted, implemented, or chosen, don't change the plan without including everyone involved in the plans conception.

**In conclusion,** as a leader, your decisions shouldn't be expected to be correct 100 percent of the time. What should be expected is an easily defined thought process behind your decision. This is a powerful tool to analyze your mistakes, failures, and successes. By adopting this you will improve mistakes, limit failures, and repeat successes.

## SWOT Analysis

A SWOT (strength, weakness, opportunities, threats) is an auditing tool used to show possible direction for an organization while helping to define the culture, mission, and vision. It also may be used to focus any team on key issues. Knowing your organizations, teams, and your own strengths and weaknesses will help you guide your team in the most productive ways.

To improve anything, or anyone, you must first have a clear understanding of what needs improving. Begin by distributing copies of the SWOT Analysis Form (See below) to your team. After all have completed the survey, schedule a meeting to discuss the following:

- What strengths need to be maintained, built upon, or leveraged?

- What weaknesses need to be remedied, changed, or stopped?

- What opportunities need to be prioritized, built on, and optimized?

- What threats need to be countered, minimized?

# SWOT Analysis Form

An answer is not required for every question. Hopefully a few questions will spur ideas and begin the thought process.

Name (please print) _____

Department _____

Date _____

**Strengths**

- What do we do well?

- What advantages does our organization have?

- What resources do we have — money, equipment, creativity, customer base, etc.?

- What are our strengths, by individual, department, or companywide?

- What is outstanding about our business?

- What do we do well that with a little improvement could be a real strength?

- What are our most competitive products or services?

**Weaknesses**

- What are obvious areas for improvement?

- What do we do badly?

- What areas need immediate improvement?

- Based on our past mistakes, what should we avoid in the future? What else should be avoided?

**Opportunities**

- What are interesting trends?

- What has recently changed that is new in our industry or new to us?

- What strengths open up new opportunities?

- What weaknesses, through development, could lead to opportunities?

- What niches have our competitors missed?

- Are there new technologies that the company can use to innovative?

- What can we do that no one else does or does, as well?

- Where can we find or create a competitive edge?

**Threats**

- What obstacles do we face?

- What and who is our competition?

- What internal or external processes are changing?

- Could one of our weaknesses be a serious threat? How can we neutralize that threat?

- What are our competitors doing better than we are?

- Are there negative political, economic, or technological trends that may hurt us?

**Combinations**

- How can we use our strengths to enable opportunities we have identified?

- How can we use our strengths to overcome threats?

- What do we need to do to overcome identified weaknesses in order to take advantage of opportunities?

- How will we minimize weaknesses to overcome threats?

- How can our strengths help overcome, reduce, or eliminate our weaknesses?

- What weaknesses expose the greatest threat and how do we improve the weakness?

- What threats could reduce our opportunities?

- What opportunities could overcome threats?

# Final Thoughts on Problem Solving

When I was younger I wanted every problem to go away. I thought how much easier my life would be without problems. I still catch myself thinking this way occasionally, but I've learned to embrace problems. Problems present an opportunity to make improvements. They can be a learning experience. And besides — they're never going away, so wouldn't it be wiser to embrace them?

Speaking of problems, time is a big one — there's just not enough of it, is there? Next let's spend some time on — time management.

# Time Management

## Chapter Twelve

# CHAPTER TWELVE: TIME MANAGEMENT

As a new manager your responsibilities, and therefore, the demands on your time, will increase; if you've been able to keep up with tasks, to be timely in your previous position but without good time management strategies — you may find the additional management activities a strain. As a manager, it's critical, to use your time wisely by applying good time management techniques. Regardless of how competent you are in your new position, using your time unwisely can be a formula for failure. If I were discussing the wise use of corporate funds, you would agree with me that unwise use of organizational monies could lead to failure. It's the same with time. Just like money we *spend* time. Spend it wisely.

To improve your use of time, you must be brutally, honest in analyzing your time usage. Let's look at some time wasters and consider where you lose time.

## Time wasters

Last month, while reviewing goals with a sales consultant, we identified time management issues. After reviewing the time wasters and savers listed below, she picked one to embrace over the next 30 days. She's ready to pick another. Rome wasn't built in a day. If you'd like to improve your time usage, read the following and choose one to begin. Starting small is better than not starting at all.

### Interruptions

Interruptions at any time, especially during "golden hours," before deadlines must be met, should be limited. To limit interruptions determine your most important times of the day, or set time aside as deadlines occur when interruptions should be limited, then consider the following:

- **Smalltalk and chitchats** can be quickly and politely ended by explaining, "That sounds interesting, could we talk later? I'm in the middle of…"

- **Work-related questions** and requests during critical times may be limited by asking these questions: Does this require my guidance? Could another team member handle this as well or better, and do they have time to do so? Do I need to do this now, and if not, when is the best time to accomplish this?

- **Establish a time and system to take messages** from team members, vendors, and clients so as not to be interrupted during your golden hours.

- **Don't waste others' time.** Are you the initiator of the interruptions? Are you respectful of your team's time?

Many team leaders spend too much time seeking solutions to a problem when someone else on the team is better suited for the task. Interruptions take time away from planned projects. Diverting oneself from a project then coming back to it takes time to refocus, which often leads to errors, adding time to the project. It's like reading the same sentence again after an interruption. It's like reading the same sentence again after an interruption. (So shoot me — I think I'm funny — now where were we?) As I was saying, interrupting a project with lower priority tasks is a poor use of time.

While interruptions may seem brief, they can add up over time. Think about it: if you have just one five-minute interruption every hour, in a standard eight-hour work day you've lost 40 minutes of time with nothing productive to show for it. Interruptions can be limited by learning how to politely and professionally diffuse them and determining your most important times of day, and most significant activities, then set time aside when interruptions are frowned upon.

### Procrastination

Are you putting off more and accomplishing less? Have you tried time management tools, like daily planners, but feel like you're getting nowhere? (Does this sound like a commercial?) Do you want to understand why you procrastinate?

- **Make decisions,** indecision leads to procrastination. Everyone has the fear of making bad choices; however, you must not let fear stop you from making a decision. Gather information, ask for input, and make a decision.

- **You aren't perfect.** You shouldn't be expected to be right all the time. What should be expected is a thought process, or the reasoning behind the decision. Do you suffer from perfection paralysis? If you cannot do it perfectly — you don't do it at all. Stop! Sometimes...you'll make the wrong decision. It. Is. Inevitable. Embrace the likelihood of being wrong as an opportunity to learn.

- **Have the courage to learn from your mistakes.** If you had a plan that didn't succeed, analyze the plan and learn from your mistakes. Most of us avoid decisions, because nobody wants to be wrong. You aren't alone. Everyone is afraid of making a poor decision. Do your homework first, and make the best decision you can based on the information available, because making no decision is a decision, and probably a poor one.

- **The Gumption Factor** is defined as beginning and completing the least attractive, most demanding task first. Try it — the feeling of accomplishment is wonderful. Procrastination can be the byproduct of a lack of prioritization. We all put off tasks that are not as enjoyable as others. How are you prioritizing tasks? What tasks take priority? Are they important tasks, urgent tasks, or simply the tasks you enjoy? What tasks and activities have been postponed? Do the tough stuff first!

- **Understand the stress you create by procrastinating.** The stress of procrastination can interfere with production, to the point of becoming a time waster — especially when it's caused by indecision, and the indecision process is recycled amplifying the stress.

  Procrastination is seldom a time-management problem; it is a thought process problem that affects time management. Improving the decision making process is integral to overcoming procrastination, Joseph Ferrari, PhD., associate professor of psychology at DePaul University in his post, "Psychology of Procrastination: Why People Put Off Important Tasks Until the Last Minute" [www.apa.org/news/press/releases/2010/04/procrastination.aspx] states, "Telling someone who procrastinates to buy a weekly planner is like telling someone with chronic depression to just cheer up!"

As a new manager, you have additional responsibilities. If you've ever been plagued by procrastination, it will be magnified in your new position — not only due to the increased work load but how your procrastination affects your direct reports. Understanding and controlling procrastination is critical to successfully managing any operation.

### Lack of or Poor Planning

The proverb, "He who fails to plan, plans to fail," warns us of the significance of planning to our success. Poor, little, or no planning is also a huge time waster. Tackling even the smallest projects without proper planning may add unnecessary time and energy. Daily planning, such as a to-do list, will save time in the long run.

Having clear team goals, and the required training to reach those goals, improves planning. The same can be said for policies (what), procedures (how), missions (why), and vision (where are we are going). If your team doesn't have this in place, establishing them will help focus the team's plans on the desired results.

- Make time to plan daily.

- Tie plans to goals.

- Use or establish policies and procedures.

- Set realistic time frames. Unrealistic time frames may lead to rushing the project, which often leads to errors.

- Clean up your office. Messy work areas and useless, outdated papers, piled high, may interfere with the planning process (Do you really need those notes from 2007?)

## Time Savers

- **Follow Daily and Weekly Routines.** Many reoccurring activities can be scheduled for the same time daily or weekly. A consistent calendar of repeated activities will eliminate energy and time wasted on fitting these activities into the schedule. Consistently scheduling these activities helps your team be prepared and available. It becomes routine.

- **Plan every day.** Some find it better to begin their day organizing their work area and creating a daily plan, others prefer to take a few minutes at the end of the day to plan for tomorrow. It doesn't matter when you do plan — what matters is taking a few minutes to plan the day.

A to-do list is the frame work of your daily plan.

Have you ever forgotten a task? Have you found yourself spending time on low-priority tasks and not getting to the important ones? Have you been surprised by an approaching deadline? If so, you may need a to-do list. Whether you use a legal pad, Outlook, or the latest hand-held device isn't important; what's important is to make and use a to-do list daily. A to-do list is a powerful tool that reduces stress and utilizes time and resources more efficiently.

**Begin a daily to-do by listing:**

- Pre-scheduled routine activities.

- List continuing projects.

- Note new projects.

- Rank assignments.

- Schedule follow ups.

- Make planning time.

The object isn't to plan every activity; it's to list every activity.

Consider these additional points when planning.

- Grade the activities by importance from A — requiring immediate attention, to F — not sure if it requires my attention. If there are too many A's demote a few and re-prioritize as needed.

- Plan more than you think you can achieve. Parkinson's Law [www.economist.com/node/14116121] states, "Work expands so as to fill the time available for its completion." Keep in mind, uncompleted low-priority tasks may be moved to the next day.

- Divide large tasks into more manageable components.

- Consider chronos time, the amount of time needed to complete the activity and Kairos time, the best time to schedule an activity.

- Plan start and stop times for each activity.

- Delegate appropriate activities. A friend asked, "How do I know what I can delegate, how do I deal with my crushing need to be in control of everything and my secret knowledge that my subordinates will screw the assignment up?" Great question, it's a fear I have often shared. These questions are answered a few pages ahead under delegation.

## Still Having Problems?

- **K-I-S-S** — Keep It Simple, Stupid!

- **List priorities**, and don't increase the list until you begin accomplishing those daily.

- **Start** a, "I'm keeping track of this" list for continuing projects.

- **Remove items** (or move them to the tracking list) that are out of your control.

- **Make a weekly list** and a separate daily to-do list.

- **Create a to-don't list**. Eliminate unimportant tasks, and delegate tasks better suited to others.

I can't overstate the importance of rewarding yourself as tasks are completed. Simply crossing off a task can be an effective **reward.** The feeling of accomplishment sends positive molecules throughout your body preparing you to successfully take on the next project. Rewards may include a break, time to work on pet projects, or 10 minutes of yoga...you get the idea.

**What if your supervisors keep giving you more than you can accomplish?** Show them your workload, your to-do list, and politely ask, "Which tasks should take priority and which should I put off?"

## To-Do List Check List

- How is it prioritized?

- Can it be delegated?

- Are urgent tasks prioritized ahead of important tasks? How many urgent tasks are on the list?

- How much time is set aside for planning?

- How does the to-do list incorporate a daily and weekly routine? How much of the list repeats daily?

- Is it portable? How is it used throughout the day?

- How are accomplishments "checked off?" How do you reward yourself?

## Delegation

Do you think you have to do it all, and then complain there aren't enough hours in the day? You may need to consider improving your delegation skills. The more team members you trust to complete projects to your satisfaction, the more successful, committed, and satisfied your team will be. Oh, and BTW, you'll have more time to concentrate on important tasks.

### Let Go

But what if you don't want to let go? You're responsible, what if they mess up? Or…how will it be perceived if they do well without you? Consider your limitations. You can only do so much efficiently. If you try to do it all yourself, you'll either take on more than you can accomplish or limit what you take on — either way you'll be seen as someone who doesn't get the job done. But if you train a team to be an extension of yourself (and more) you may be perceived as a true leader — someone who improves the talent around him or her.

Start by giving your staff expectations. Share your decision making criteria. For example, if you gather information from several sources before making a decision share the procedure — don't assume your team will do the same without your direction.

- What organizational policies and procedures do they need to know?

- What activities do they need to learn?

### Next, Provide Your Team with Direction

- When are the results expected?

- What activities will achieve these results?

- What authority does the team have to engage these activities?

### Don't Give up When They Mess Up

Are you perfect? Stop playing the blame game. When the outcome of delegation is not what you'd hoped for, you should consider what you could've done in the delegation process to improve the results.

- Delegate gradually, beginning with smaller short-term objectives before moving to larger ones.

- Set a reporting schedule. Don't wait until the project is completed to check it. Check the project throughout the project's timeline.

- Let team members make decisions. If they are at an impasse offer pros, cons, and alternatives, do your best to let them make the decision.

- Enable failure by congratulating the team's understanding of the failure. Give them confidence allowing them to implement procedures to prevent future failures.

- Consider delegating tasks you're good at — you can give direction, advice, and training.

### Don't Cause Failure By Delegating The Following:

- Projects with a high risk of failure.

- Employee reviews (it's not their job.)

- Reprimands or demotions.

### Someone May Be Better Suited Than You

In "The Art of Delegation," [https://www.coursehero.com/file/27274803/The-Art-of-Delegationpdf/] Gerard M. Blair, uses the example of a janitor responsible for emptying the trash bins. If you tell the janitor to empty the bins on Tuesday and Friday, the bins will be emptied on Tuesday and Friday. If the bins overflow on Wednesday, they will be emptied on Friday. If instead, you said, "empty the bins as needed," the janitor would decide how often and adapt to special circumstances. You might suggest a regular schedule, but by leaving the decision up to the janitor, you apply his/her local knowledge to the problem. Consider this — do you wish to be an expert on emptying trash bins, and can you devise instruction that covers all contingencies? If not, delegate this to someone who is paid for it.

Until you learn to delegate you not only limit your potential but hold back learning opportunities from your team, which reduces the effectiveness of both.

## Controlling the Ping

Email and social media can be a tremendous distraction and time killer. We are becoming a society of ADHD squirrel chasers. We allow pings to pull us away from what we're doing, interrupt our activities, and slow us down. It's difficult not to; that ping delivers an adrenaline rush. It validates our importance and our connectedness. To control correspondence, email, social media, and text you need to determine the minimum time required daily to respond. For example, I don't work directly with customers, employees, or vendors in urgent situations; therefore, I can check my email three times daily — morning, after lunch, and at the end of the day. To help me with this, I've turned off notifications. If your work is urgent, if a customer needs an answer now, if a vendor must verify your order before shipping, or an employee needs an answer to maintain the workflow, you may not be able to divorce yourself from every ping. However, you can limit the interruptions by determining if the interruption should take priority over the activity you're currently doing rather than automatically jumping to the ping.

Whenever possible email and other correspondence should be handled as they're opened always striving for inbox zero at least by the end of the day.

## The Urgent vs. Important Dilemma

Are your priorities confused? Is there no one who can do it as well as you? Do you have to do it? Why is that? It could be how you're prioritizing tasks.

- **Urgent tasks** are "sudden fires" that do little to achieve long-term goals, and may interfere with them.

- **Important tasks** are those that help achieve the long-term individual and team goals.

I worked with a team leader, who, along with many of his responsibilities, had the important task of processing customer invoices. The invoicing process was slow and mistake-prone partly due to "urgent" interruptions that "only he" could handle. When I suggested he should stop to consider, "Do I need to do this, and do I need to do this now?" More often than not, he was able to work on the important task of properly invoicing clients, instead of running to the urgent emergency, putting out the fire "only he" could correct. Are you spending too much time putting out fires instead of doing your job?

**Before jumping to an urgent task that "only you" can do ask yourself:**

- Who should do this?

- When should it be done?

- If I complete this task now, what tasks are being interrupted, set aside, or left incomplete?

- Will this task help achieve my goals?

- Does this task interfere with my goals?

- What tasks should take priority?

The next time you spend two hours putting out urgent fires instead of completing your planned activities, stop and consider — are you working toward your long-term goals, or are you operating by the seat of your pants? Are you working on the business or in it?

# Additional Time Management Suggestions

- Cut down caffeinated beverages; often the burst of energy is outweighed by the crash when the caffeine wears off.

- Don't overthink. Always look for ways to simplify projects and activities. Simple is elegant.

- Keep your work area clean and organized. Studies show junk mail at home is a significant source of stress. It's the same at work. If it's junk, throw it away, don't make piles. Not only does a sloppy work area slow down work — If a customer, banker, client, saw the work area would it impress them about the organization? What if someone else needs to use the area or find something?

- Handle it, don't shuffle it.

- Exercise revitalizes; amazingly it doesn't diminish the energy supply it enhances it. Try 10 minutes of stretching, walking, or any exercise in the middle of a busy day. When it feels like nap time, try 10 minutes of activity.

- Don't commit to meaningless tasks. A job may seem inconsequential or may be off in the future, however, if it doesn't help your team reach their goals, develop team spirit, or help the organization, it may be a waste of time. It's OK to say no. When you agree to too many projects, stop and think about the projects you won't be able to complete. Make sure you are following you and your team's priorities, not the priorities of others.

## Do You Micro-Manage?

One of the overlooked consequences of micro-managing is poor time usage. Micro-managing can be a huge time drain. Learning to overcome those tendencies will free you to pursue the more important task of developing a team to grow your department or business.

Are you a micro-manager? If you say, "yes" to any of the following bullet points, you may be micro-managing yourself out of a loyal, passionate, productive team and wasting time.

### Signs of Micro-Managing

- Believing, "If I want it done right, I've got to do it myself."

- Taking over projects before they're completed.

- Changing how things are done to fit your way, even when existing systems are adequate.

- Not allowing others to make decisions.

- Monitoring even the smallest details of projects.

- Distrusting others abilities.

- Lack of delegation.

### Failures Of Micro-Managing

When people aren't allowed to make decisions or mistakes, they don't grow. Don't waste the most valuable resource you have — people. Logic dictates your organization will struggle to improve if it ALL depends upon you. The de-motivation, resentment, and fear created by micro-managing will weaken your organization. Although micro-managing may work occasionally, in the long run it will hinder growth and reduce performance.

### Stop Mis-Managing through Micro-Management

Within limits, allow others to make mistakes. If they have a legitimate thought process behind their decisions, it will be a learning experience. Right or wrong, it can help the team improve. By explaining your decision to let them go forward, despite any reservations you may have, and reiterating the importance of their thought process you allow direct reports to think and act outside of the box without setting them up for failure.

Instead of taking over, or doing it yourself, **teach someone to do it.** Better yet, take a deep breath, explain the result you desire, and ask your team how they will accomplish the result. If progress is made and, deadlines are being met — why would you get involved? If the quality of production is up to standards, and policies are being followed, don't interfere.

When team members come to you for a decision, **ask their opinion** Give your team the authority to make decisions. While attending a trade show, I watched an unhappy customer approach an exhibit and confront a young staff member. The representative did a great job of listening to the customer and regaining their trust. She ended by offering a free product to the customer. After the satisfied customer had left, I asked the staff member who had given her the authority to offer free merchandise? She said the president of the company had empowered her to, "Do what he would do."

As a leader, you're not paid to *do* the work; you're paid to *get the work done.* You probably were one of the best at accomplishing tasks, but now your responsibility is to teach others, not to do it all yourself. How do you stop micro-managing? Start by reviewing your job description. It probably doesn't call for you to do the work, but rather to manage the people who do the work. Ask for direction from your leaders. Remember to work *on* the business, not *in* it.

# Time Management Inventory Form

1. Time management areas to improve

   a. _____

   b. _____


2. Strategies from time wasters and time savers to utilize

   a. _____

   b. _____

   c. _____

   d. _____

3. Start date _____

   Review date _____

   Deadline _____

4. Summary at conclusion

   _____
   _____
   _____
   _____
   _____
   _____
   _____
   _____
   _____

# Delegation Outline

Clearly Define the Project

_____

_____

_____

Appoint the Project Team and Leader

_____

_____

_____

State the Results Expected

_____

_____

_____

Set a Completion Date

_____

_____

_____

Plan a Reporting schedule with Follow up Date

_____

_____

_____

Define Team authority

_____

_____

_____

Make a Plan of activities

_____

_____

_____

## Have We Spent Enough Time on Time?

I've spent a lot of time on time haven't I? I hope it wasn't overkill or a source of intimidation because the truth is we all waste time. If you picked up a few time management strategies either adding time savers or reducing time wasters you're ahead of the game. Time management isn't something you learn once and go on to the next class, but continues throughout your career. Improving time efficiency is part of the search be an effective leader, which leads us to the question...What is leadership?

# What is Leadership?

## Chapter Thirteen

# CHAPTER THIRTEEN: WHAT IS LEADERSHIP?

What makes a leader and can leadership skills be developed?

As I've previously shared, the key ingredient of being a leader is a sincere desire to help others. Some will disagree with me and say job skills and knowledge are the most critical attributes for leadership. Let me share a story. As VP of Operations for a B2C organization I was thrown into a position managing a large installation and service team. The VP of installation had suffered a debilitating stroke and no one was prepared to take his place. I had never installed the product and only knew enough about it to be dangerous. What I did know...was how to lead a team. I wanted to help them, and the company. I stayed in that position for over a year. During that time we won national awards for customer service, lowered our service response time, and developed a comprehensive training program, which allowed us to hire for character. But my greatest achievements were developing and assisting in the development of a future vice president, several managers, and watch employees purchase their first homes, get out of debt, and improve their lives. Enjoying helping others may not be the only useful leadership character trait, but it's been the most common I've observed among successful leaders. Leadership is service.

## Attributes of a Leader

- Leaders share vision and give direction.

- Leaders show character and integrity.

- Leaders constantly strive to improve themselves.

- Leaders set high standards and raise the bar.

- Leaders plan for growth.

- Leaders take responsibility.

- Leaders make decisions.

- Leaders set the example.

- Leaders share information and keep teammates informed.

- Leaders know their team.

- Leaders mentor, train, delegate, and listen.

- Leaders give recognition at every possible opportunity.

## Leadership Is Service

I've heard those words for years, but never understood them until I found myself outside looking in. My title at TKO Graphix is "Director of Communications"…we're still figuring out what that means; however, like many in small to mid-sized businesses I wear several hats. Along with my communication responsibilities, I'm privileged to work on leadership training. I've recruited, interviewed, and been part of the hiring process, and I help manage the sales team. The thing is — I have zero direct reports. For the first time in 30 years, I "manage" no one…but I do lead. Outside looking in, not being a manager, I believe I've become a better leader. Although I don't manage anyone directly, I have a vested interest in many of my teammates, and from this perspective, it's easier to see the most effective leaders are leaders who serve.

- **Set Your Ego Aside** — Let's face it, part of why you became a manager is ego, but ego will often get in the way of effective leadership. Others are best served when ego is set aside.

- **People Are More Important Than Projects** — When anyone manages a project, it's almost natural to focus more on the plan than how team members fit the plan. However, success may depend more on how team members *execute* the plan than the plan itself. Don't make people fit a plan; make a plan that fits your people.

- **Help Someone Everyday** — As a manager of direct reports, it's easy to get lost in the day-to-day battle and forget the big picture — the more you help members of your team, the more cohesive and loyal the team will be.

- **Seek Advice from Others** — When you're putting out fires, it's easy to forget to seek input. By involving others in the plan, you may improve the plan and support of the plan. Involve others; make team plans, not *your* plans.

- **Share Everything You Know** — There should be little that is on a need-to-know basis; if it's useful, share it. Help others avoid mistakes, pitfalls, and problems. Teach others what has worked for you.

Service is not intangible; it's giving, caring, and sharing. The best leaders are leaders because people matter to them. As a leader, there's no greater reward than watching others grow, in part, due to the leader's direction and influence. A true leader is not served — a true leader serves. Whom have you served today?

# What Makes an Attractive Leader?

Projects and paperwork are managed, but people are led. If we lead well — people will follow. The title doesn't make a leader. A leader is someone others want to follow. If you want to attract followers learn to be...

- **Someone who has both the employees' and the company's best interests at heart.** Setting expectations and offering the training to hit goals makes for a leader people will want to follow... Sharing a vision and a plan — even more so. When a leader can get the job done, show pride in the work, and have fun doing it, they are almost irresistible.

- **Someone who readily hands out recognition.** Recently, a manager bragged to me about a member of his team, describing in detail how they took initiative. I asked the manager how the employee reacted when he was told this. The employee hadn't been told. If you want people to repeat positive activities — recognize the behavior.

- **Someone they can talk to — who listens.** Don't make this complicated — listen to ideas and keep an open mind. That's it. While it's a compliment to be asked to listen to your teammates' non-work related concerns — don't let it interfere with getting the job done. Unless they directly affect work, consider taking non-work related conversations to lunch or after hours.

- **Someone who includes all teammates within the team.** If you want to build a team, make every member part of the team. Seek input, ideas, and advice. Promote plans as team initiatives by involving the team in the planning. If you want followers, don't just tell people what to do, but show them how to do it and explain why it's done that way.

- **Someone who treats others fairly.** Don't confuse equal with equitable. Fair doesn't have to be equal, but should be equitable. Don't play favorites, but if tenured teammates deserve consideration because of their accumulated contributions — give it to them. It would be unfair to treat a dependable, tenured teammate the same as an unproven new employee.

- **Someone who sets a good example.** Keep in mind; your direct reports will often copy your weaknesses before they copy your strengths. Believe me, they watch and learn. Teach them traits you admire through your actions. If you relish team members with character traits such as dependability, loyalty, honesty, attentiveness, and thoroughness — demonstrate those characteristics to your team.

Leadership is service. It's about giving, not taking. To be a leader, you must attract followers. To attract followers, people must know you care. Your direct reports should be more efficient because of your leadership, not the other way around. Do you help others become better at what they do? Are you someone others want to follow because they know they can count on you? Ask yourself, "Would you follow you?"

**Leadership Axioms**

- An organization's most valuable commodity is its people.

- It's not who's right; it's what's right.

- The most common outcome to verbal communication is misunderstanding.

- Help comes from empathy, not sympathy.

- Personal recognition and being a part of a team are important ingredients of job satisfaction.

- Don't make your problems your customer's problem. Under-promise and over-deliver.

- Don't dwell on what *can't* be done; concentrate on what *can* be done.

- Don't dwell on what you *cannot* control; concentrate on improving what you *can* control.

- If people didn't need leadership, guidance, and direction, no one would need managers. Don't expect your team to do it on their own without supervision.

- Don't base communication on the assumption others think as you do — they may not.

- Don't assume others learn like *you* learn. Learn how *they* learn. Train how *they* learn.

- You don't need to be close friends to work together efficiently; you are expected to be best teammates by respecting and supporting each other.

- Don't silo. Work together to reach peak performance.

- Eliminate the word "worry" from your vocabulary. Replace "worry" with "concern." Concerns fit one of two categories; you can do something about it, or you cannot.

- Too often, we tell others how the clock was built when they only asked what time it was.

# Are You Working ON or IN Your Business?

It's easy to convince yourself you're doing what's best for the organization when you're working long, hard, productive hours, and completing tasks — but is what you're doing truly in the best interest of the organization? It depends.

- Do you want to grow?

- Is your organization positioned for growth?

- Who in your organization can do what you do?

- What's holding you back?

If you have no one in your organization that can do what you do, your growth is limited. If you want to grow then you must train someone to take on your job, which allows you to take on other responsibilities.

During a seminar at Indiana University's Kelly School of Business, the lecturer asked a room full of entrepreneurs and executives the following question: "When it's time to add an employee to help grow your business, would you hire someone who has knowledge or skills you share, or someone who has knowledge you don't?" His answer surprised many "Hire someone to replace you." With this practice, you can learn other competencies and grow the business. Besides, if you don't understand what someone is doing, how would you know if they're effective? Learn how to do it — GROW your company. I'm not naive enough to believe you can train yourself to be an attorney or a rocket scientist. If you need specialized professional advice, you'll need to depend on others, but look around your organization; **who** can replace you? Who can do what you do?

Working IN the Business is:

- Doing tasks others can do.

- Not training others what you know.

- Not hiring to replace you.

- Busy putting out fires rather than assigning firemen.

- Letting results manage you.

Working ON the Business is:

- Delegating and following up.

- Training, training again, training more.

- Mentoring.

- Overseeing — not overdoing.

- Developing systems and procedures.

- Planning and sharing visions.

If you want to grow your organization, you must be the director, not the actor. What do you want to be?

# The 7 Most Important Business Questions — Ever

The questions you ask your customers, clients, and prospects aren't the most important questions. The most important questions are the ones you ask yourself beginning with, "What have I learned?"

### Check-in With a Checklist

Budget 30–45 minutes at the end of your workweek to review your activities and consider opportunities for improvement.

- **Review activities to repeat.** Success is not luck; when results are favorable, ask — what did I do and what can I repeat?

- **Identify areas to improve.** The first step to improvement is identifying what needs improving. After you've identified areas of improvement, consider the best method of improvement. Can you improve through self-help, or is a more experienced person available to mentor?

  o What was my most successful activity last week?

  o How can my successful activities be repeated?

  o What, within my control, was my biggest time killer?

  o What activity didn't work and why?

o   What do I need to stop doing?

o   What do I need to improve?

o   What's my improvement plan?

When I was a very young man, I was asked what I wanted to improve about myself. My answer was — I hadn't thought much about it. I was given the assignment of identifying three things about myself I wanted to improve. Then I was asked to jot them on a slip of paper, put them in my wallet, and look at them daily. By being directed to concentrate on these areas, I was forced to consider how I might improve. Years later, I consider these former weaknesses to be strengths.

As I've said before, and will say again without activities any goal is a wish. Learn from your failures and your successes. If you ask yourself these seven questions every week, reflect, and act on them — you WILL improve.

## Leadership Means Putting Others First

If you're in a leadership position within an organization, it doesn't stop at the office. As painful as it is to admit, I'm nowhere near the leader or person I hope to be. I've recently had three different interactions with friends in which my actions were disappointing, and with less than desirable outcomes. What did they have in common? My "ME FIRST" attitude — I *acted* on "ME first," because my *thoughts* were of "ME first." I wasn't listening to, understanding, or considering the wants and needs of others. Yep, I was pretty disappointed in myself. So after apologizing and wallowing in self-pity, I decided to do something about it. I need to improve on putting others first — do you?

- **Listen Better.** My listening skills are challenged at best. To put others first, I'm concentrating on what they have to say, not so much about what I want to say. Asking open-ended questions helps.

- **Be More Considerate.** These words are so common; I think they've lost their meaning. Being considerate means thinking about what others want and need and how my actions may affect their desires.

- **Think Past the Moment.** What may seem appropriate for the moment may not be, when viewed through a wider lens. I ask myself, "How important is this and what are the consequences of my actions?"

- **Set Ego Aside,** this is my Achilles heel. It's the big one. I want things to go my way because...*I'm special*. I want to share information and show how knowledgeable I am, even if it hurts others; I seldom hesitate to disparage others if I think it will get ME a laugh. I'm working on setting my ego aside; besides...self-deprecation is in-style, isn't it?

When your actions are thoughtless and hurtful, an apology never brings back the time lost in regret; by the time you realize what you've done, it can be too late. It would be unrealistic to think I'll never put myself in this position again — I will. But I can work towards reducing it, can't I? In the long run, putting others first is in my best interest, AND theirs. Leaders put others first. Be a leader 24/7.

## What Will Get You...Unfollowed as a Leader

To understand why some people are followed, you need to know why some people aren't. People will seldom follow you just because you have a title. They may follow your instructions if you have the power to affect their career, but that's not following a leader. Following a leader means having belief and trust in the leader's vision.

- **They will not follow you only for money.** A small percentage may, but most people need more. Followers follow because they know what they're doing is right; it has purpose. It means something, and they want to make a difference.

- **They will not follow you just because of your charisma.** Don't get me wrong — people may be attracted to your charm, but they won't continue to follow if you lack substance. Followers want to know what you're made of; they want leaders of character.

- **They will not follow you if you're self-serving.** Leaders who serve themselves and not their followers eventually have no one to lead. Followers want to know how you will help them. They will not follow you because you said so. The quickest way to lose people is to shout, "DO WHAT I SAY not what I do." Leaders lead by example.

- **They will not follow you if you're mean-spirited, gossipy, negative, and vindictive.** If you treat others poorly, people know you may eventually do the same to them. Followers want leaders who respect others.

## Leadership Credo

A few years ago, my good friend, Rene Reed, and I wrote the following leadership credo to introduce a leadership development course. Its contents are nothing new. It's what we've always thought was true and meaningful. It's what we believed good leaders followed, and it still holds true today.

- Treat others with respect.

- Maintain integrity and adhere to your code of ethics. Commit to giving your best effort at all times. Embrace personal accountability, rather than looking to place blame with others.

- Show a commitment to excellence in customer service.

- Be the best teammate you can be.

- Strive for individual development, growth, and continuous learning.

- Rise to the challenges before you.

- Follow policies and procedures and if they don't work, improve them.

- Give expectations to others; instruct them on how to proceed, and follow-up with everyone.

- Listening is understanding — listening is wanting to hear.

- If you're unsure, ask.

- Always take notes.

- Ask others if they understand.

- Set meaningful goals and track them.

- Have fun! Laugh!

## A Few Last Words

Reading this workbook is only the beginning of your journey. In 2008, I left my full time position and began leadership development consulting. I was flabbergasted by the lack of management training and leadership development offered to managers. It wasn't limited by industry, size, geography, or type of organization. For the most part — it didn't exist. That's not to say there weren't a few organizations doing outstanding jobs of training their managers and future managers either in-house or outsourced, there just wasn't very much of it going on. My point is, learning how to be a leader may be *entirely up to you.*

# What's the Next Step?

Continue seeking. Whatever motivated you to read this workbook — keep those flames burning. Find other sources, read from great leaders (I share a few in the appendix) seek out mentors, and attend seminars, webinars, and classes.

Do NOT put this guide away in some drawer or closet. Put it on your desk and review it as you plan activities. You won't agree with everything, some of it will fit your personality and responsibilities — some of it won't. Use what works for you. Scribble notes all over it, scratch out what doesn't fit you or the job, and add what does. Becoming more than a manager of projects but a leader of people is an ongoing never-ending task. There's always more to learn and ways to improve. Ain't it great? Welcome to the journey.

Feel free to contact me with questions. I'm also available for Leadership development seminars at your organization, but I have to warn you — I only take assignments if I understand and believe in what the organization is doing, I know I can make an impact, and most important of all — it looks fun.

Thank you, Randy

Phone 317-306-9713

Email - rclark@randyclarkleadership.com

This workbook is released under a creative commons license.

Attribution-NonCommercial 4.0 International: creativecommons.org/licenses/by-nc/4.0

# Appendix

I've not only included sites mentioned in the workbook but sites and people who have influenced, inspired, and taught me. I hope you take the time to become familiar with all of them.

Management Help.Org [managementhelp.org]

Character first [www.characterfirst.com]

Brookhaven College Learning style/Modality Test [https://webster.uaa.washington.edu/asp/website/site/assets/files/3104/learning_style_questionnaire.docx]

John Maxwell on Leadership [johnmaxwellonleadership.com]

Coach John Wooden [www.coachwooden.com]

Ken Blanchard [www.kenblanchard.com]

The Delivering Happiness Movement [www.deliveringhappiness.com/jointhemovement]

Forbes - Money Motivation [www.forbes.com/2010/04/06/money-motivation-pay-leadership-managing-employees.html]

Prezi [prezi.com]

# Acknowledgments

I want to acknowledge those who inspired and taught me what I know about leadership, and those who helped me with this labor of love. My parents Lyle and Bea owned a small business I worked in growing up where I learned many of the principles I continue to use. I was fortunate to be mentored by the late Jerry Heir, he taught me about leadership and life. Joe Schuette and Bob Dillon taught me more than I could put in one book. My co-workers Josh Humble and Nancy Jarial have read and edited much of what I've written, there's a place in heaven for them. Eric Benge is responsible the illustrations, and Andy Hollandbeck did the formatting and the overall design, making this workbook a *work of art*. My dear friend Allison Carter not only edited the manuscript, but added over 500 comments, questions, and ideas — not all of them were flattering, which was exactly what I needed. Both my daughters, Dawna and Amanda, patiently listened as I bounced ideas off of them and picked their brains and last, but not least, my loving wife Cathi helped me in more ways than I can list. Thank you all.

# About the Author

Randy Clark retired as the Director of Communications at TKO Graphix, where he continues to blog for TKO Brandwire, so he can concentrate on his passion — leadership development. He can be found blogging about leadership on his site RandyClarkLeadership.com. He's the proud father of two educators, grandfather of four amazing grandchildren, and husband to a wife who devotes her time to helping others.

He resides in Speedway, Indiana, and on weekends can be found performing rock 'n' roll with the Under the Radar band, hiking, flower gardening, or sharing an IPA.

Made in the USA
Monee, IL
21 August 2021